FINDING JOY IN THE WORD
BY RENEWING THE MIND

SET YOUR MIND ON THINGS ABOVE

ANDREW ZINK

CONTENTS

CHAPTER 1

FINDING TRUE HAPPINESS

"You will show me the path of life; in your presence, there is fullness of joy; at your right hand are pleasures forevermore."
(Psalm 16:11)

No matter who we are or where we've been, we're all looking for happiness in some form or another. But the problem arises as to where or who we go to find that happiness. Some look to drugs and drink; others look to people and places. But, like the great Saint Augustine said, "God has created us for Himself. Our hearts are restless until we find our rest in Thee." We all have that "hole in our soul" when we look to anything and everything else aside from our Creator to fill that void. Somewhere deep inside, we know we were created for so much more. But then, as we go on trudging through life, that feeling starts to dissipate, and we just learn to numb it.

As many of us know, our true spiritual battle between good and evil, God and the devil, mostly takes place within our minds. And the discipline of renewing our minds to The Word of God is one of the most important things as believers that we can ever do. As Romans 12:2 states:

***"Do not be conformed to the pattern of this world, but be transformed by the renewing of your mind. Then you will*

*be able to test and approve what God's will is—His good,
pleasing, and perfect will."***

The Greek word for "transformed" is where we get the word "metamorphosis" from. So, like the caterpillar, we do not become bigger and better caterpillars, but rather become a new creature through Christ (2 Corinthians 5:17).

When we first gave our lives to Christ, our spirit and redemption were sealed. However, our minds still have the same old tapes playing in us from before we were saved. But by renewing our minds to God's Word, we can truly live out the abundant life that Jesus promised in John 10:10. The whole goal of this book is to help you do just that. By renewing our minds and fighting the good fight of faith, we will not only find greater peace and joy, but we will also make the devil and his demons shudder! Through the Holy Spirit and The Word, we can win the greatest battle that's ever been fought! But we have to be intentional about it, and I will help you do just that in the chapters to come.

We all know the story of David and Goliath. But just like every word in the Bible, even the tiny details we might gloss over matter. One detail being that "David ran 'quickly' to the battle line." Most things in life are out of our control. But in the area of renewing the mind, only through Christ do we have control over our thoughts. So, like David, let's run quickly to the battle line and wage war in our minds! God is good. You got this!

DIVE DEEPER:

Read Romans 12:2.

1. Why is it so important to renew our minds?

2. Choose one stronghold that you are currently dealing with as you go through this book.

3. What are some of the ways you have tried to find happiness other than through God? Does it really bring you happiness in the end?

THINK ON THESE THINGS:

Try to memorize and meditate on Psalm 16:11.

KEY THOUGHT:

When you think better, you feel better and live better. There is nothing greater to think on than The Word of God.

POWER PRAYER:

Dear Lord, please forgive me when I have looked to anything and everything else aside from You for my supreme happiness. Your gifts are amazing, but there is no greater gift than You. Please help me read, meditate, study, breathe, and live Your Word like never before so my life can be a testimony of Your goodness and grace to whoever You place in my life. In the precious name of Jesus. Amen.

CHAPTER 2

STRANGLING STRONGHOLDS

THE BATTLE IS THE LORD'S!

L et us begin.

For the weapons of our warfare are not of the flesh but have divine power to destroy strongholds. We destroy arguments and every lofty opinion raised against the knowledge of God and take every thought captive to obey Christ (2 Corinthians 10:4-5).

The Greek word "ochuroma" Is the origin of the word "stronghold" in the Bible. It is a noun that means a fortress, castle, or citadel. It can also mean anything that someone relies on, such as arguments or reasonings. I can't think of a greater story to demonstrate a stronghold than Adam, Eve, and the serpent Satan in the Garden of Eden. The devil uses the same exact tactics today as he did in the beginning. And I hate to admit it, but his plan "can" still be quite effective to this day. If it still works, why would he change his approach? But the great news is that through Christ and renewing our minds to The Word, we no longer have to buy into the lies from the father of lies himself!

It Is also just as important to note that he tempted Eve the same way he tempted Jesus. However, as we know, while Eve lost the battle, Jesus shut it down with The Word of God and was victorious. And we can do exactly the same. Just as Eve and Our Lord did, we too deal with the same three temptations: the lust of the flesh, the lust of the eyes, and the pride of life, which are not of the Father but of the world (1 John 2:16).

Let us jump into a few verses of Genesis chapter 3:

"Now the serpent was more subtle than any beast of the field which the Lord God had made. And he said unto the woman, 'Yea, hath God said, Ye shall not eat of every tree of the garden?' And the woman said unto the serpent, 'We may eat of the fruit of the trees of the garden: But of the fruit of the tree which is in the midst of the garden, God hath said, Ye shall not eat of it, neither shall ye touch it, lest ye die.' And the serpent said unto the woman, 'Ye shall not surely die: For God doth know that in the day ye eat thereof, then your eyes shall be opened, and ye shall be as gods, knowing good and evil.' And when the woman saw that the tree was good for food, and that it was pleasant to the eyes, and a tree to be desired to make one wise, she took of the fruit thereof, and did eat, and gave also unto her husband with her; and he did eat."

One of Eve's biggest mistakes (which we have probably all made at some point or another) was having a conversation with the killer, as Pastor Louie Giglio has stated. It's important to note that we should never talk to the devil. The moment we do that, we lose the battle. We talk only to God but rebuke the devil with the Word. Satan threw in the infamous "what if" or, in his case, "did God really say." He knew fully well what God had instructed Adam and Eve, and they did too originally. But like the original sin of the Bible from Satan himself, Adam and Eve were also compelled by the sin of pride. He made Eve feel that God was holding something out on her. We too may feel that God is holding something out on us. But He only "holds out" on things that would hurt us and even destroy us.

So, when it comes to renewing our minds, the devil throws the same fiery darts (thoughts) today as he did in the beginning of time. It is very important to know that we do not always have control over what thoughts come into our minds; however, we do have full control over what thoughts stay in our minds. I believe it was Martin Luther who said it best: "We cannot keep the birds from flying over our head, but we can stop them from building a nest in it." In order to defeat the strongholds in our minds, we must know the Truth of The Word of God. As Jesus said, "You shall know the truth, and the truth will make you free" (John 8:32). Now, the Truth that Jesus spoke of was first and foremost Himself and His Word. But it is also the truth about ourselves in Christ to destroy the lies we have and still believe about ourselves. The only way to counter these strongholds is to study and know The Truth of The Word and apply it to our lives.

Remember that no matter how we "feel," The Word is always true. So, when you hear thoughts like "I am a complete failure," you automatically reject that thought and go to The Word that says, "I am a blood-bought child of Christ, and He loves me so much that He died for me!" The more and more we study and meditate on The Word, the easier it will be to recognize the lies of the enemy. And more importantly, the more we study and apply The Word, the more we learn the Truth that will set us free!

Just like our great Savior and Lord, when faced with every temptation, we will fight back the powers of hell by saying, "It is written!" (Matthew 4:4-6). In order to speak what is written, we must know what is written and also think on what is written.

Keep this Book of the Law always on your lips; meditate on it day and night, so that you may be careful to do everything written in it. Then you will be prosperous and successful.

So let's dig into true Biblical meditation in the next chapter!

DIVE DEEPER:

Read 2 Corinthians 10:4-5

- Like Adam and Eve, do you ever feel like God is "holding something out" on you? If so, why?

- To help identify a stronghold if you are not already aware: What is the first thing that comes to mind when you think of something you "can't" live without?

- What is the number one way God speaks to us?

THINK ON THESE THINGS:

Try to memorize and meditate on 2 Corinthians 10:4-5.

KEY THOUGHT:

If a thought doesn't line up with the Word, reject it immediately so it doesn't grow.

POWER PRAYER:

Dear Lord, please help me through Your Holy Spirit to take every thought captive that is contrary to Your Word. And please fill my mind with Your Word and Your Word only. In the Name above all names, Jesus. Amen.

CHAPTER 3

RENEWING THE MIND

Do not be conformed to the pattern of this world but be transformed by the renewing of your mind. Romans 12:2

RENEWING YOUR MIND TO THE WORD OF GOD

In the journey of faith, one of the most transformative processes one can undertake is the renewal of the mind through the Word of God. The Bible, as the inspired and authoritative source of divine wisdom, provides us with the guidance and spiritual nourishment necessary for this renewal. In this chapter, we will explore the significance of renewing your mind to the Word of God and practical steps to achieve it.

THE IMPORTANCE OF RENEWING YOUR MIND

The mind is a powerful instrument that influences our thoughts, emotions, and actions. It's the battleground where spiritual warfare takes place. Romans 12:2 (NIV) urges us:

- "Do not conform to the pattern of this world, but be transformed by the renewing of your mind. Then you will be able to test and approve what God's will is—his good, pleasing and perfect will."

1. **Transformation**: Renewing your mind is a process of transformation. As you saturate your thoughts with God's Word, you begin to align your thinking with His truth. This transformation shapes your character and decisions.

2. **Discernment**: A renewed mind helps you discern God's will and distinguish it from worldly influences. It equips you to make decisions that honor God and reflect His values.

3. **Spiritual Growth**: Renewal is central to spiritual growth. Just as a plant needs sunlight and water to thrive, your spirit needs the Word of God to grow strong and healthy.

PRACTICAL STEPS FOR RENEWING YOUR MIND

1. **Daily Devotion**: Set aside dedicated time each day for reading and meditating on the Bible. Start with a passage that speaks to your current circumstances or struggles. Reflect on its meaning and how it applies to your life.

2. **Memorization**: Committing key verses to memory helps you internalize God's Word. When faced with challenges, these verses become readily available in your mind, offering guidance and comfort.

3. **Study and Reflection**: Dive deeper into the Scriptures through study. Utilize study Bibles, commentaries, and online resources to gain a better understanding of historical and cultural contexts. Journal your insights and revelations.

4. **Prayer**: Prayer is a vital component of renewing your mind. Seek God's guidance and ask Him to illuminate His Word as you read. Pray for wisdom and understanding.

5. **Community**: Engage with a community of believers who share your commitment to renewing the mind. Discussing Scripture, sharing insights, and holding one another accountable can be a powerful support system.

6. **Renewal of Thoughts**: Continuously evaluate your thought patterns and attitudes. Are they in alignment with God's Word? Identify areas where you need transformation and seek God's help in renewing your thinking.

7. **Application**: Apply what you learn from the Word of God to your daily life. Put your faith into action by living out its principles, even when faced with challenges.

8. **Patience and Perseverance**: Renewing your mind is a lifelong journey. Be patient with yourself, and don't be discouraged by setbacks. God's grace is sufficient to carry you through.

THE FRUIT OF RENEWED MINDS

As you commit to renewing your mind to the Word of God, you will experience the transformative power of His truth. Your thoughts will become increasingly aligned with His will, your decisions more reflective of His wisdom, and your life a testimony to His grace. This renewal is not a one-time event but a lifelong process that deepens your relationship with God and equips you to live a life that honors Him.

In conclusion, renewing your mind to the Word of God is a profound and essential aspect of your Christian journey. It empowers you to break free from the conformity of the world and walk in God's truth. As you faithfully engage with His Word and seek His guidance, you will find renewed strength, discernment, and a deeper connection with your Creator.

DIVE DEEPER

Read Proverbs 23:7

- What do you believe the author is saying in this verse?

- Do you believe that changing your thought life to the Word can change your life? Why or why not?

- How does Biblical meditation differ from Eastern meditation?

- Look up the Hebrew and Greek definition for the word "meditate."

THINK ON THESE THINGS

Try to memorize and meditate on Proverbs 23:7.

KEY THOUGHT

True Biblical meditation is not about emptying ourselves or "being one" with ourselves. Rather it is filling ourselves with the Word of God to be one with Him.

POWER PRAYER

Father, renewing my mind to Your Word can be so challenging sometimes. But with You, all things are possible. Please help me to meditate daily on Your Word to be transformed into the person You created me to be so I can live and love like never before. In Jesus' Name, Amen.

CHAPTER 4

DELIGHTFUL DISCIPLINE

 # DISCIPLINE AND JOY IN MEDITATING ON THE WORD

"No discipline seems pleasant at the time, but painful. Later on, however, it produces a harvest of righteousness and peace for those who have been trained by it." – Hebrews 12:11

One of the biggest problems in our world is that we have too many choices and more distractions than ever before. As the famous inventor Blaise Pascal wrote, "All of humanity's problems stem from man's inability to sit quietly in a room alone." Most of life is about perspective. If we approach the Word of God as a mindless duty to check off our list for the day, not only will we have no passion to repeat it, but we will also gain nothing from it. However, if we approach it as God's written Word, knowing that every answer we need for all our life's problems is contained within it, we will not only look forward to it, but we will look forward to it with great joy. The most important benefit we gain from meditating on the Word is getting closer and closer to the Creator of the universe. There is no greater joy than that! (Matthew 24:35)

In order to reap the benefits of the Word and get closer to Jesus, we must be disciplined about it. I know discipline can be a scary word for most people. But if we set in our minds what that discipline will produce, we can start to see it as a joy rather than a duty. I love how Pastor Craig Groeschel put it: "Discipline is choosing what we want most over what we want now." When we think about the simple act of eating, we never even think twice about putting something in our stomachs when we are hungry. But if we are that disciplined in digesting physical food, how much more disciplined should we be in digesting our spiritual food! If we hunger for the Word of God even half as much as we hunger for that nice steak dinner or whatever our food of choice may be, we would be unstoppable in our walk with God! And like any other habit, the more we practice it, the more we will want to do it. As Joshua 1:8 says,

- "This book of the law shall not depart out of your mouth, but you shall meditate on it day and night, that you may be careful to do according to all that is written in it; for then you shall make your way prosperous, and then you shall have good success."

What an amazing promise we are given in that verse! By meditating, speaking, and living the Word, we will be prosperous and successful. And this verse does not speak of worldly success, although that can happen. It speaks of godly success, which far surpasses anything that this world can offer! In other words, you can never go wrong by applying the Word to your life. Does that mean we will never have troubles in this life? No, as Jesus stated,

- "I have said these things to you, that in Me you may have peace. In the world you will have tribulation. But take heart; I have overcome the world" (John 16:33).

Despite all the trouble and heartache we may face, we have something far greater. We have the Creator of all on our side as we walk through this crazy world. And He promised that He will never leave us or forsake us! So let the troubles come, but also know that our great Lord has overcome all of them, and through Him, we can have joy even in the midst of our trials. A joy that the world can never strip from us. Joy unspeakable. So, like the Apostle Paul stated near his departure, we too can say,

○ "I have fought the good fight, I have finished the race, I have kept the faith. Finally, there is laid up for me the crown of righteousness, which the Lord, the righteous Judge, will give to me on that Day, and not to me only but also to all who have loved His appearing" (2 Timothy 4:7-8).

I am quite confident that if you are reading this book, you are tired of listening to the lies of the enemy. Let us, through diligence and discipline, take back what the enemy has stolen by renewing our minds to the Word of God! And let us do it with great joy!

DIVE DEEPER

Read Hebrews 12:11

○ Would you rather go through the pain of discipline for a greater joy or go through the pain of regret?

○ Do you look forward to reading the Word? Why or why not?

○ Would changing your mindset from "trying" to "training" give you a new perspective on studying the Word?

THINK ON THESE THINGS

Try to memorize and meditate on Hebrews 12:11.

KEY THOUGHT

The pain of discipline is worth the end result.

POWER PRAYER

Lord, please give me a hunger for Your Word like never before. Help me understand that even though I may feel pain at first doing things Your way at times, the end result is worth far more than any pain I ever endure. In the precious name of Jesus, Amen.

CHAPTER 5

THINK IT, SPEAK IT, BREATHE IT: THE PATH TO PEACE: EMBRACING POSITIVE BIBLICAL THINKING

Finally, brothers and sisters, whatever is true, whatever is noble, whatever is right, whatever is pure, whatever is lovely, whatever is admirable—if anything is excellent or praiseworthy—think about such things. Phillipians 4:8

As we continue our journey through the powerful teachings of the Apostle Paul in Philippians, we arrive at a pivotal passage that implores us to shape our minds in a way that fosters inner peace and spiritual growth. In Philippians 4:8-9, Paul offers us profound guidance on how to achieve this transformative change in our thinking.

- **Verse 8**: Finally, brothers and sisters, whatever is true, whatever is noble, whatever is right, whatever is pure, whatever is lovely, whatever is admirable—if anything is excellent or praiseworthy—think about such things.

- **Verse 9**: Whatever you have learned or received or heard from me, or seen in me—put it into practice. And the God of peace will be with you.

In these verses, Paul encourages the believers in Philippi to embrace a mindset that is rooted in positivity, truth, and righteousness. Let us break down these guiding principles and explore how they can be applied to our daily lives.

1. **Whatever is True**: The pursuit of truth is essential for a noble mindset. In a world filled with falsehoods and misinformation, it is our responsibility to seek and hold onto what is genuinely true, both in our faith and in our interactions with others.

2. **Whatever is Noble**: Nobility in thought and action speaks to the idea of holding ourselves to a higher moral standard. It encourages us to be honorable, virtuous, and dignified in our dealings with others.

3. **Whatever is Right**: Righteousness is at the core of a life well-lived. We are called to align our thoughts and actions with what is morally right and just, even when faced with adversity.

4. **Whatever is Pure**: Purity is about maintaining an untainted heart and mind. To achieve this, we must guard against impure thoughts and influences that can lead us astray.

5. **Whatever is Lovely**: The beauty of life can often be found in the simple, lovely moments. By focusing on what is lovely, we can cultivate gratitude and joy, even in challenging circumstances.

6. **Whatever is Admirable**: Cultivating admiration for the good in others fosters unity and love. It encourages us to look for the best in people and situations.

7. **Anything Excellent or Praiseworthy**: Excellence and praiseworthy actions should be celebrated and emulated. By

recognizing and acknowledging these qualities, we inspire growth and positive change in ourselves and others.

In Verse 9, Paul reminds us that these principles should not remain theoretical but must be put into practice. It is not enough to merely think about these things; we must live them out in our daily lives. By doing so, we open ourselves up to the transformative power of God's peace.

As we embrace these principles, we find that they are not merely a list of dos and don'ts but a roadmap to a life filled with inner peace, joy, and the presence of the God of peace Himself. Through positive thinking rooted in truth, nobility, and righteousness, we unlock the profound promise of spiritual growth and a closer relationship with our Creator.

May we, like the believers in Philippi, strive to embody these teachings in our lives, knowing that the God of peace will walk with us on this transformative journey!

DIVE DEEPER

Read Philippians 4:8-9

- On an index card or app, write out each attribute in verse 8. Then next to it, write something that aligns with that attribute. So next time your thoughts are running in a negative direction, pull this list out.

- Think about what you are thinking about right now. Do you like where these thoughts have been taking you? Why or why not?

THINK ON THESE THINGS

Try to memorize and meditate on Philippians 4:8-9.

KEY THOUGHT

If I can ruminate on the negative, I can surely ruminate on the positive. With God, all things are possible.

POWER PRAYER

Lord, please forgive me when my thoughts don't line up with Your Word. But more importantly, please help me line up my thoughts with it. I only want to think on what is lovely, true, just, pure, and praiseworthy in the mighty name of Jesus. Amen.

CHAPTER 6

SPIRITUAL WARFARE WIELDING THE SWORD OF THE SPIRIT

Ephesians 6:12 reminds us:
"For we do not wrestle against flesh and blood, but against the rulers, against the authorities, against the cosmic powers over this present darkness, against the spiritual forces of evil in the heavenly places."

As we dive into spiritual warfare, there are a few very important things to know. One is that, no matter how much we may believe or even want to believe that our fight is with each other, it is not. That is not to say that people are not held responsible for their actions. Also, there are just some people that we have to make healthy boundaries with or steer clear of, as Psalm 1 states:

"Blessed is the one who does not walk in step with the wicked, stand in the way that sinners take, or sit in the company of mockers, but whose delight is in the law of the Lord, and who meditates on His law day and night" (Psalm 1:1-3).

"

However, our ultimate battle is against The World, The Flesh, and The Devil. The Bible refers to the world in two ways. As the famous John 3:16 says, "God so loved the world." So if our enemy is the world and God loves the world, how does that make sense? It is because when God refers to the world in that verse, He is speaking of the people in the world – you and me. When the Bible speaks of the world as our enemy, it is referring to the systems of the world, the status quo. A great example would be the ways of Hollywood, but that's a whole other topic for another book. But suffice it to say, there are two definitions of the word world in the Bible.

Another very important thing to clear up is that God and Satan are not on equal grounds. Sadly, there are many out there who still believe this. And I shamefully admit that when I was a baby Christian, I thought it as well. But make no mistake, God is the creator and Satan is just another creature He created.

"You were blameless in your ways from the day you were created, till unrighteousness was found in you"
(Ezekiel 28:15).

So let us never forget that God is greater than all. And also let's remember that Satan is on a very short leash as he knows his days are numbered and will eventually be no more!

The last thing I would like to bring up on spiritual warfare in this text is that we don't want to fall to either end of this spectrum. One spectrum is where we believe everything and anything is of the devil and his demons. We definitely don't want to give him any more credit than he thinks he has. But just as important, if not more, is that we don't go to the other end of the spectrum and completely deny his existence. In fact, I believe that is one of the devil's greatest tricks! Because if we don't believe he exists, how do we know who and what to fight against?

With that being said, I'd like to draw attention to our great Savior in the wilderness. If we ever plan on defeating Satan, then we must learn from the Best of the Best of the Best! It is so important to know exactly what Jesus was doing before the Spirit led Him into the wilderness.

THE BIBLE READS:

"As soon as Jesus was baptized, he went up out of the water. At that moment heaven was opened, and he saw the Spirit of God descending like a dove and alighting on him. And a voice from heaven said, 'This is my Son, whom I love; with him I am well pleased'" (Matthew 3:16-17).

So, as you know, this was at the beginning of Jesus's mission. There are so many great things drawn out of this verse that we can meditate on. Notice that God was well pleased with Jesus before He even did anything in His mission! So all of us who feel like our lives are only based on our performance, please meditate on that verse! Also, notice this was God's public blessing and declaration of His Son: "This is My Son."

Now let's go to the wilderness. Notice the first thing the tempter said to Jesus: "If you are the Son Of God." This is literally right after God made a public announcement to the world, which I'm sure Satan was very well aware of, saying "This is My Son in whom I am well pleased." So, needless to say, the devil knew what he was doing. And he does the same to us today. He attacks our identity in Christ:

"Well, if you were a Christian, you wouldn't...?"

"You are no child of God..."

"He doesn't love you..."

"Who are you anyway?..."

"Lies, lies, and more lies."

Let us contrast how Eve and Jesus dealt with the same temptations, and why Eve lost and Jesus overcame.

Once again, with Eve, Satan began with a question doubting God's love for Eve and her identity in Him: "Did God really say?" Then Eve started questioning what God had told her and even engaged in conversation with the devil. The moment we start questioning God's Word is the moment we lose the battle.

Now let's look at how our Savior dealt with that very same temptation. The tempter came to him and said, "If you are the Son of God, tell these stones to become bread."

Jesus answered, "It is written: 'Man shall not live on bread alone, but on every word that comes from the mouth of God.'"

Unlike Eve, notice Jesus did not question Satan's temptation at all, nor did he engage in conversation. Rather He went straight to the Word: "It is Written." So if Jesus Himself used the Word to defeat Satan, how much more should we use it!

"For the word of God is living and active, sharper than any two-edged sword, piercing to the division of soul and of spirit, of joints and of marrow, and discerning the thoughts and intentions of the heart" (Hebrews 4:12).

The Word, as you may know, is also called The Sword Of The Spirit. It is important to know that the "sword" Paul refers to, uses the Greek word machaira, which typically means a short sword or even a dagger, although the word is used throughout the New Testament as the go-to word for a sword, whatever the context. So we are not speaking of a huge Goliath-type sword which is used at a distance. We are talking about a very up close and personal dagger when engaged in battle. So this is a personal fight we are involved in when the devil hits us with his fiery darts.

There is no greater way to learn and know the meaning of a book and its application than from the author Himself. In the Bible's case, we have The Great Counselor. The Holy Spirit, the paraclete, is Παράκλητον, and 'spirit' is Πνεῦμα (pneuma), meaning 'breath.' Pneuma appears over 250 times in the Christian

New Testament and is the word used to refer to the Holy Spirit, i.e., the Spirit of God. As we study and renew our minds to God's Word, the Spirit breathes life into them and makes them alive and active!

The devil may be able to pull the wool over our eyes but has never and will never fool the Holy Spirit. So with the Word and the Spirit's guidance, we can finally demolish the strongholds of the devil and his demons and take victory, just as our Great Lord did in the wilderness!

"It is Written, It is Written, It is Written!"

I'd like to end this chapter with some lyrics by the infamous musician Bobby Dylan. Whether you like his music or not, you have to admit he was a genius writer. This is an excerpt from his song "Let Me Die in My Footsteps." While you read, imagine the great confidence we can have in Christ through spiritual warfare and all walks of life!

"I will not go down under the ground cause somebody tells me that death's coming around. I will not carry my self down to die; when I go to my grave, my head will be high. Let me die in my footsteps before I go down under the ground. Through Christ and all of us together, let's die in our footsteps before we go up to the sky!"

DIVE DEEPER:

Read Matthew 4:1-11

- What was the first thing the devil attacked Jesus with?

- How did Jesus fight this battle?

- If Jesus used the Word to defeat Satan, how much more should we use it?

THINK ON THESE THINGS:

Try to memorize and meditate on Ephesians 6:12.

KEY THOUGHT:

The Word has the power to slay the enemy.

POWER PRAYER:

Dear Lord, as I fight this spiritual battle, please help me wield the Sword of the Spirit (The Word of God) at all times, so I can take back the ground the enemy has stolen. In Jesus' name, Amen.

CHAPTER 7
NEW SOUNDTRACK

"Finally, brothers and. Sisters, whatever is true, whatever is noble whatever is right, whatever is pure, whatever is lovely, whatever is admirable—if anything is excellent or praiseworthy—think about such things." (Philippians 4:8-9).

I am positive it has happened to us all at some point. But have you ever had one of the worst but most catchy songs stuck in your head on repeat? You totally disdain the song but yet you can't stop playing it in your head! That is exactly what our minds are like apart from The Word of God!

Some experts say we have 30 to 60+ thousand thoughts that go through our minds every day! I can't stop thinking about how many thoughts that is! Okay, so make it 60+ thousand. But seriously, if we are being honest with ourselves, how many of those thoughts line up with The Word? No judgment whatsoever, but we have so many negative voices in the world nowadays.

But now picture the time where you have had one of your favorite, most amazing songs on repeat in your head. Tell me how amazing that makes you feel! That's what it is like to have our minds on The Word but an Eternity times greater!

"Set your minds on things above, not on earthly things."
(Colossians 3:2).

In this verse, Paul is not talking about having your mind on cloud nine every day. But rather looking at everything through a Biblical perspective, which makes cloud 9 look like cloud 6 or 7. The more we meditate on what is true, what is honest, what is lovely, not only will our lives become far more joyful, but more importantly, we will start to think like Jesus!

"But we have the mind of Christ (the Messiah) and do hold the thoughts (feelings and purposes) of His heart."
(Isaiah 40:13).

As we practice renewing our minds, this is an area we have to be intentional about. God will definitely help us. But no one else can do this for us. But I am fully persuaded the more and more we do this, the more and more we will want to do this.

So let us, with great perseverance, turn off the old soundtrack in our minds and start jamming the new one! Just like anything else, technology can be used for God or evil. At the same time we can look at pornography and other ungodly ventures, we also have almost unlimited access to The Word and godly things, which means we have a plethora of ways to digest The Word!

So turn on your favorite sermons or crank your favorite worship songs. But most importantly, spend time with God in His Word, and I guarantee you'll be playing the greatest soundtrack you have ever heard!

DIVE DEEPER:

Read Colossians 3:2

- What does it mean to set your mind on things above?

- According to this chapter and the Bible how do we do that?

- What are some things you have set your mind "below" on?

- Did those things ever truly bring you peace and joy?

THINK ON THESE THINGS:

Try to memorize and meditate on Colossians 3:2

KEY THOUGHT:

When we set our mind on things above we can never go wrong

POWER PRAYER:

Lord, please help me set my mind on things above and keep it set so I never turn back to things behind. In Jesus name. Amen

CHAPTER 8
SPEAK THE WORD

"Death and life are in the power of the tongue: And they that love it shall eat the fruit thereof." (Proverbs 18:21).

We all know the old saying, "sticks and stones will break my bones, but words will never hurt me." Well, along with many other false sayings that have become ingrained in our memories, this is definitely one of the worst! Just as important as it is to think on and meditate on The Word, speaking The Word has dunamis

(Greek translation), dynamite power! In fact, many of the proverbs, along with many other books in the Bible, teach us that the way we use our words is one of the most prevailing subjects.

With our words, we can either lift someone from the depths of hell or we can send them down there! Of course, I was being figurative, but needless to say, our words are very powerful. In fact, the book of James says:

"When we put bits into the mouths of horses to make them obey us, we can turn the whole animal. Or take ships as an example. Although they are so large and are driven by strong winds, they are steered by a very small rudder wherever the pilot wants to go. Likewise, the tongue is a small part of the body, but it makes great boasts. Consider what a great forest is set on fire by a small spark. The tongue also is a fire, a world of evil among the parts of the body. It corrupts the

whole body, sets the whole course of one's life on fire, and is itself set on fire by hell. All kinds of animals, birds, reptiles, and sea creatures are being tamed and have been tamed by mankind, but no human being can tame the tongue. It is a restless evil, full of deadly poison." (James 3:3-7).

Man, we can definitely do a lot of damage with our words! But the beautiful news is that the more we meditate, think, and breathe The Word, the more our mouths will line up with our minds! And also, the more we speak and hear The Word, the more we will get it in our thoughts!

"So then faith cometh by hearing, and hearing by the word of God. But I say, Have they not heard? Yes verily, their sound went into all the earth, and their words unto the ends of the world." (Romans 10:17).

Just to demonstrate the power of our words, please try this. In your mind, start counting up to four:

One..Two..Three..Four, and on the Three, just shout "Hallelujah!" Notice how it interrupted your thoughts?! There is power in the tongue!

I remember when I was a kid; I used to silently judge that old crazy guy on the street who was always talking to himself. But as I've grown and continue to grow in Christ, I've come to the conclusion that I've been wrong all these years, and maybe they knew something I didn't. That is if they were actually, as the Bible says of David,

"He stirred himself up in The Lord." But now I love being that "crazy" guy on the street! Now I don't suggest that in every public place you should be shouting out loud everywhere you go. However, there is definitely a time for that! But I definitely suggest and highly recommend that you walk and talk with God everywhere you go!

So next time you have a million negative thoughts spiraling in your head, try speaking or shouting The Word out loud! And as God Himself said:

"So shall My word be that goes forth from My mouth; It shall not return to Me void, But it shall accomplish what I please, And it shall prosper in the thing for which I sent it."
(Isaiah 55:11).

So in Christ, let's get our mouths moving with The Word, and we can all become like that "crazy" guy on the street and walk and talk in the way of our Great God!

"Now go, and I, even I, will be with your mouth, and teach you what you are to say." (Exodus 4:12).

DIVE DEEPER:

Read Proverbs 18:21

- In what ways has your tongue brought death to yourself or someone else?

- In what ways has your tongue brought life to yourself or someone else?

- Pick one person on your heart today and speak life to them.

THINK ON THESE THINGS:

Try to memorize and meditate on Proverbs 18:21.

KEY THOUGHT:

Our tongues have tremendous power, so we should choose our words wisely.

POWER PRAYER:

Father, please help me speak only life with the tongue you gave me, to others and myself according to Your Word. In Jesus' Name. Amen.

CHAPTER 9

PRAY THE WORD

Praying with the Word of God: Speaking Life and Blessings

INTRODUCTION:

In this chapter, we will explore the transformative power of praying with the Word of God. The act of praying Scripture back to God, not only helps us connect with Him in a deeper way, but it also allows us to speak life and blessings over our lives and the lives of others. As we delve into this topic, we will learn practical ways to incorporate this practice into our daily prayer life and witness the amazing results it can bring.

1. *The Power of Praying Scripture:*

    The Bible is not merely a book of stories and teachings; it is a living Word that carries great authority and power. When we pray with Scriptures, we align ourselves with God's truth, inviting His wisdom, guidance, and blessings into our lives. By praying His Word, we express our trust and faith in His promises and invite Him to work In and through us.

2. *Finding the Scriptures:*

    Finding the right Scriptures to pray may sometimes seem overwhelming, but it doesn't need to be. Start by identifying specific areas in your own life or the lives of others where you desire God's intervention, healing, or guidance. Then, search the Bible for verses that address those needs. Bible concordances, topical study

Bibles, or even utilizing search engines can help you find relevant passages.

3. *Personalizing the Scriptures:*

   Once you have identified the Scripture verses that align with your prayer needs, personalize them. Meditate on the meaning of the verse and how it applies to your specific situation. As you internalize the truth and promises within these verses, allow the Holy Spirit to show you how to incorporate them into your prayers in a personal and genuine way.

4. *Praying with Authority and Confidence:*

   As we pray with the Word of God, it is important to remember that we are operating in alignment with God's will. This gives us the authority and confidence to boldly approach His throne and claim His promises. When we pray God's Word, we can be assured that He is listening and responding according to His perfect plan.

5. *Speaking Life and Blessings:*

   When we pray with the Word of God, we speak life and blessings over ourselves and others. By declaring the truths and promises found in Scripture, we are sowing seeds of faith, hope, and love into our lives. As we intercede for others, we release God's power and blessings into their lives, ushering in transformation and breakthrough.

6. *Examples of Praying with the Word:*

   To help you get started, here are a few examples of how you can incorporate praying with the Word in your

PRAYERS:

- *Pray for strength:* "Lord, your Word promises that those who wait on you shall renew their strength. I lean on this promise now and ask for your strength to sustain me in my weakness."

- *Pray for healing:* "Father, your Word assures us that by Jesus' stripes, we are healed. I claim this promise of healing over my body and trust in your restorative power."

- *Pray for wisdom:* "God of wisdom, in your Word, you promise that if any of us lacks wisdom, we should ask you, and you will generously give it. Grant me discernment and clarity in the decisions I need to make." – Pray for guidance: "Heavenly Father, your Word declares that you will guide us along the best pathway for our lives. I seek your guidance and ask for your direction in the choices and paths before me."

7. *The Transformational Impact:*

As we consistently pray with the Word of God, we will experience a transformative impact on our lives. Our faith will grow stronger, and we will witness God's faithfulness and provision in ways we never thought possible. Our prayer life will become more intimate, and our relationship with God will deepen as we align ourselves with His truth and promises.

CONCLUSION:

Praying with the Word of God is a powerful practice that enables us to connect with God on a deeper level, speak life and blessings into our lives, and invite His transformative power into our circumstances. As we incorporate this practice into our daily prayer life, we will witness the amazing results of aligning our prayers with God's Word. Let us never underestimate the power of praying with the Word of God, for it has the ability to bring about supernatural breakthroughs and incredible blessings in our lives and the lives of others.

DIVE DEEPER:

Here is the edited version formatted for Microsoft Word:

DIVE DEEPER:

Read Proverbs 18:21

- In what ways has your tongue brought death to yourself or someone else?

- In what ways has your tongue brought life to yourself or someone else?

- Pick one person on your heart today and speak life to them.

THINK ON THESE THINGS:

Try to memorize and meditate on Proverbs 18:21.

KEY THOUGHT:

Our tongues have tremendous power, so we should choose our words wisely.

POWER PRAYER:

Father, please help me speak only life with the tongue you gave me, to others and myself according to Your Word. In Jesus' Name. Amen.

CHAPTER 10
LOVE THE WORD

Loving the Word of God: Nourishment for the Soul

INTRODUCTION:

In this chapter, we will explore the importance of loving the Word of God and how it can nourish our souls. The Bible is not just a book of ancient texts, but a living and breathing treasure that holds immense wisdom, guidance, and love from our Heavenly Father. By cultivating a deep love for God's Word, we can experience spiritual growth, discover God's heart, and find direction for our lives. Let us delve into the beauty of loving and cherishing the Word of God.

THE WORD AS A BEAUTIFUL GIFT:

The Bible is a remarkable gift from God to humanity. It contains His thoughts, His heart, and His will for our lives. Just as receiving a gift from someone we love brings joy and excitement, we can approach the Word of God with anticipation and gratitude. Recognizing the Bible as a treasure will fuel our desire to explore and understand its contents.

1. *Seeking Divine Revelation:*

   When we approach the Word of God with a heart that yearns for divine revelation, we position ourselves to encounter the living God. The Scriptures hold the power to transform our lives and reveal God's character and plans. As we ask the Holy Spirit for understanding and illumination, the words on the page come alive, speaking directly to our hearts.

2. *Feeding on the Word:*

In the same way that our bodies require nourishment to thrive, our souls hunger for spiritual sustenance. The Word of God provides the perfect food to satisfy our spiritual hunger. Just as we savor a delicious meal, we can savor the depth and richness of Scripture, allowing it to fuel our faith, renew our minds, and invigorate our spirits.

3. *Meditating on the Word:*

Meditating on the Word involves more than casual reading; it requires intentional reflection and contemplation. As we meditate on Scripture, we allow God's truth to sink deep into our hearts. Taking the time to ponder and internalize His Word enables us to apply it practically in our lives and experience its transformative power.

4. *Obeying the Word:*

Loving the Word of God involves more than simply studying and reflecting upon it. True love for God's Word is demonstrated through obedience. As Jesus taught, "If you love Me, keep My commandments." (John 14:15) Obedience is an act of love and trust, showing that we value God's Word and believe it to be the ultimate guide for our lives.

5. *Sharing the Word:*

When we love something, we naturally desire to share it with others. The Word of God is meant to be shared, as it has the potential to bring hope and transformation to those who hear it. As we share the Scriptures with others, we can speak life, encouragement, and truth into their lives, inviting them to experience the same love and transformation we have found in God's Word.

6. *Scripture Coordination:*

Here are a few Scripture passages that highlight the beauty and significance of loving the Word of God:

- Psalm 119:11: "I have hidden your word in my heart that I might not sin against you."

- Psalm 119:105: "Your word is a lamp for my feet, a light on my path."

- Joshua 1:8: "Keep this Book of the Law always on your lips; meditate on it day and night, so that you may be careful to do everything written in it. Then you will be prosperous and successful."

- Hebrews 4:12: "For the word of God is alive and active. Sharper than any double-edged sword, it penetrates even to dividing soul and spirit, joints and marrow; it judges the thoughts and attitudes of the heart." – James 1:22: "Do not merely listen to the word, and so deceive yourselves. Do what it says."

CONCLUSION:

Loving the Word of God is an invitation to intimately know and experience our Heavenly Father's heart. As we cultivate a deep love for the Scriptures, we find nourishment for our souls and guidance for our lives. Let us treasure the Word of God, seeking divine revelation, meditating on its truths, and obeying its commands. May our love for the Word overflow, compelling us to share its life-giving message with others. By embracing and cherishing the Word of God, we embark on a remarkable journey of spiritual growth, transformation, and divine encounter.

DIVE DEEPER:

Read Psalm 119:11

- What does it mean to hide God's Word in your heart?

- What is the best way to do that?

- Read Psalm 119:105.

- How has God's Word been a lamp to your feet and a light to your path?

THINK ON THESE THINGS:

Try to memorize and meditate on Psalm 119:11.

KEY THOUGHT:

The Beatles were right about one thing: "All we need is love."

POWER PRAYER:

Dear Lord, please help me love Your Word by living Your Word, and please help me live Your Word by loving it. In Jesus' Name. Amen.

CHAPTER 11

LIVE THE WORD

"But be doers of the word, and not hearers only, deceiving yourselves." (James 1:22).

Everything we have gone through thus far is eternally important. However, I hate to say, we could do all that – knowing the Word, studying the Word, meditating on the Word – but without applying the Word, we will never enjoy the fruits of our labor!

Don't get me wrong, all those things are great perils, but as James writes:

"What does it profit, my brethren, if someone says he has faith but does not have works? Can faith save him? If a brother or sister is naked and destitute of daily food, and one of you says to them, 'Depart in peace, be warmed and filled,' but you do not give them the things which are needed for the body, what does it profit? Thus also faith by itself, if it does not have works, is dead. But someone will say, 'You have faith, and I have works.' Show me your faith without your works, and I will show you my faith by my works. You believe that there is one God. You do well. Even the demons believe—and tremble! But do you want to know, O foolish man, that faith without works is dead?"

In these verses, James is by no means saying that we are not saved by faith and faith alone. But rather he is saying if our faith is genuine, we will naturally characterize the fruits of our faith by good works. It is also so important to know that these works are not by any means to "get" God to approve of us. As Isaiah 64:6 States:

"But we are all as an unclean thing, and all our righteousnesses are as filthy rags; and we all do fade as a leaf, and our iniquities, like the wind, have taken us away."

But rather we do these works because God has "already" approved of us when we first came to Jesus, and because of what The Word says in 1 John 4:19:

"We love him because he first loved us."

I am a firm believer that Biblical thinking can and does lead to Biblical actions. But I have also heard a great saying that definitely has profound truth to it as well. Sometimes we have to act our way into right thinking. I believe a big reason why most of us at some time or another have a hard time taking that first step is because of a fear of stepping out into the unknown. But if we are truly being honest with ourselves, I believe the root fear is wondering if God can be trusted and if what He says in His Word is actually true. Because like many of us, whether we realize it or not in all our chaos, we still sometimes think, "I can figure this out myself." But if that were so, we would have done that a long time ago.

I don't say any of this to heap any more condemnation on ourselves than we already put on ourselves. In fact, it's the complete opposite of condemning. It's a convicting truth that runs throughout The whole Word Of God that when we finally come to the end of ourselves, that's when we come to find our true selves in Christ.

"Anyone who loves their life will lose it, while anyone who hates their life in this world will keep it for eternal life."
(John 12:25).

So, as I stated at the beginning of this book, we are all searching for happiness. By renewing our mind to The Word and applying it to our lives, happiness and joy are just one of the many by-products that you will attain. But the most important benefit of these practices is getting closer to the One who saved our lives from the pits of hell!

But in order to grow closer, this is something we need to be intentional about. And not me, but the Bible itself guarantees that when we do these things, we will grow closer to God, we will treat others and ourselves better, and we will be able to finally overcome the grips of the devil and his demonic cohorts! The only thing left for us to do? In the words of Nike: "Just do it."

DIVE DEEPER:

Read James 1:22

- What do you believe is the biggest issue when you are not able or don't apply The Word? Lack of trust? Fear of loss of something important? Explain.

- What is one issue you may struggle with when it comes to applying The Word to your life? Why do you think that is?

- If you knew for sure that you would leave this world tomorrow, would it change how you live out The Word? Why or why not?

KEY THOUGHT:

Information without application does not equal transformation.

THINK ON THESE THINGS:

Try to memorize and meditate on James 1:22.

POWER PRAYER:

Lord, please help me live Your Word like never before, so I can be a testimony to Your goodness to whoever you place in my path. And help me live in Your joy all the days of my life. In Jesus' Name. Amen.

CHAPTER 12
TRUTH OR FEAR

So do not fear, for I am with you; do not be dismayed, for I am your God. I will strengthen you and help you; I will uphold you with my righteous right hand. (Isaiah 41:10)

I'm sure at some point or another you have heard the acronym for Fear: False Evidence Appearing Real. There is definitely a lot of truth to that statement. Although we definitely have many real fears, if we really pondered for a second though, we would agree that the majority of our fears are not even reality. But we can definitely believe them as if they are.

When it comes to our minds, worry and fearful thoughts are truly just a form of meditating on the negative or the unknown in our lives. But the great news about that is if we transition that meditation to the positive and more specifically The Word at that same caliber, we can truly start to live out the peace that passes understanding!

As the great Apostle Paul states,

"Do not be anxious about anything, but in every situation, by prayer and petition, with thanksgiving, present your requests to God. And the peace of God, which transcends all understanding, will guard your hearts and your minds in Christ Jesus" (Philippians 4:6-7).

To be completely honest, reading that at first you might think Paul is a little crazy.Do not be anxious about "anything"?! I sometimes think and feel that I am literally anxious about everything! We may read that and think, sure, that's Paul The Apostle, a super Saint; of course, he doesn't worry about anything. But if we take a look at Paul before his conversion, we can definitely say that he had to learn these things, and they didn't come overnight. He went from sending out orders to kill Christians to reaching the ends of the earth, sharing the Gospel of Christ! Which is amazing news for us! It truly brings such comfort to know that just about all the heroes in the Bible were screw-ups like us at times! I'm so glad to know they didn't walk this journey perfectly. If they did, I don't think there would be much hope for us in our walk.

But of course we do know One Man who walked on this earth in perfect form with perfect love. So when we come back to not being anxious about anything, we have a God who went through "everything" for us, and through Him, fear has no'power over us like it used to!

"For we do not have a high priest who is unable to sympathize with our weaknesses, but one who in every respect has been tempted as we are, yet without sin"
(Hebrews 4:15).

And it is so important to understand that you being anxious or fearful at times is in no way ever a sin. Can it lead us to sin? Absolutely. But in and of itself, it is not. It is a true tragedy to me that there are some in the pulpit who teach erroneous doctrine like that. If anxiety and fear itself were sin, all we have to do is go to The Garden Of Gethsemane with Our Great Savior:

"And being in an agony he prayed more earnestly; and his sweat became as it were great drops of blood falling down upon the ground" (Luke 22:44).

In That garden, Jesus felt and bore more anxiety and fear than we can ever imagine! However, as we know from the verse above, He suffered through all of this without any sin, and as we also know, He spoke some of the most courageous words ever spoken in the history of the world:

"He went a little farther and fell on His face, and prayed, saying, 'O My Father, if it is possible, let this cup pass from Me; nevertheless, not as I will, but as You will'" (Matthew 26:39, NKJV).

And He did this for the glory of The Father and us!

"Greater love has no one than this: to lay down one's life for one's friends" (John 15:13).

So if Jesus literally took on all sin ever committed in the whole universe and the punishment that we rightfully deserved, and was nailed viciously to The Cross but yet conquered Satan's ultimate blow of death, and rose on the 3rd day, and we have Him on our side, what is there truly ever to fear?! "There is no fear in love, but perfect love casts out fear. For fear has to do with punishment, and whoever fears has not been perfected in love." The ultimate punishment or fear is separation from God. Thankfully, for us who believe in Jesus, that fear has passed and no longer has a hold on us!

So in the beginning of this chapter, I stated that popular acronym for Fear: False Evidence Appearing Real.

Well, I'd like to change that around a bit and start casting out the fear that haunts our minds. Fear: Facing Everything After Resurrection! I have not researched it myself, but I've heard from many theologians that the words "fear not" occur in the Bible 365 times. That means we have a "fear not" for every single day of the Year!

All of us at some point in our lives have had the fear of death. Whether it be physical, emotional, or even worse, spiritual. Or all three. Death was Satan's greatest weapon. So he thought. But as we know from Acts 2:24: "But God released [Jesus] from the horrors of death and raised him back to life, for death could not keep him in its grip." Personally, that is one of the most powerful verses in Scripture! Who else but our Lord could say "death has no hold on me"?! But because of His shed blood on that Tree, we too can say the same thing! So next time you are facing any fear and it seems like there is no way out and have completely come to the end of yourself, please scream out "Because Of Jesus, death has no hold on me!".

Needless to say, Satan completely underestimated The power of our Great God! In fact, The Bible goes on to say, "He disarmed the rulers and authorities and put them to open shame, by triumphing over them in him." Our great captain has won the contest. Not only did Satan's final move completely come crashing down. But on top of it, Jesus made a public spectacle of it! This, of course, is just me paraphrasing. But I just picture Jesus saying, "You see this tough guy with all his tricks and schemes, who thought he'd finally win by sending the ultimate death blow? Well, look at him now. Not looking so good for you, buddy!" Of course, like I said, I was obviously paraphrasing and, needless to say, I don't think Jesus would ever call Satan "buddy". Lol. But the point remains that he threw out every secret weapon he had and was defeated for all the world to see. Through that, Jesus opened up the way to The Father on our behalf. And now we can say,

"I sought the LORD, and he answered me; he delivered me from all my fears" (Psalm 34:4).

Notice that verse did not say "some" or "most". It says He delivers me from "all" of my fears. I'd like to close out this chapter with something for you to meditate on. So, when fear sets in and you feel you have no courage within, please meditate on this. You have the same Spirit inside you that raised Christ from the dead! No fear and no devil in hell is any match for that truth!

DIVE DEEPER:

Read Isaiah 41:10

- What do you fear more, life or death? Why?

- What is an unhealthy form of fear? Explain.

- What is a healthy form of fear? Explain.

- What do you believe having the fear of God means?

- Although He is the Creator of the universe, should we be "afraid" of God? Why or why not?

- Look up the word reverence in the dictionary.

KEY THOUGHT:

The fear of God takes away all other fears.

THINK ON THESE THINGS:

Try to memorize and meditate on Isaiah 41:10.

POWER PRAYER:

Lord, thank you that Your perfect love casts out all fears. Let me live this day and every day with the complete confidence that with You I truly have nothing to fear. In Jesus' Name. Amen.

CHAPTER 13
IT'S TIME FOR WAR

There is a time for everything, and a season for every activity under heaven: a time to love and a time to hate, a time for war and a time for peace. (Ecclesiastes 3:1 and 9-10)

I'm sure if you have come this far in the book that you are tired of being beat down by the lies of the enemy or of the negative thoughts that may swirl through your mind every day. Or you're sick and tired of saying you're sick and tired of being sick and tired. I completely understand. I am as well. But the great news is that we don't have to live this way anymore, that there is a way to silence the lies of Satan and his demons, and we can live out the abundant life Jesus promised us.

But in order to do that, we have to get serious about this battle! The first thing we must do is to actually acknowledge that this is a battle. Everything we face in life always starts somewhere in the spiritual realm, whether good or evil. But what is so awesome is that we are given every weapon we need to disarm the powers of hell!

For though we live in the world, we do not wage war as the world does. The weapons we fight with are not the weapons of the world. On the contrary, they have divine power to demolish strongholds.
(2 Corinthians 10:1)

We cannot fight this battle the way the world would. We would lose before we even got started. There is only one way to win this battle, and that is through Jesus, The Word of God, and the Body of Christ. We must set our hearts and minds on Christ and Christ alone.

When we look at our circumstances, it will seem as if we are losing every battle we may encounter. We all know the amazing story of Jesus and Peter walking on water.

"And Peter answered him and said, 'Lord, if it be thou, bid me come unto thee upon the waters.' And he said, 'Come.' And Peter went down from the boat, and walked upon the waters to come to Jesus. But when he saw the wind, he was afraid, and beginning to sink, he cried out, saying, 'Lord, save me.' And immediately Jesus stretched forth his hand and took hold of him and saith unto him, 'O thou of little faith, wherefore didst thou doubt?'" (Matthew 14:28-31)

It's funny whe' most people preach on these verses, they always seem to focus on the part of Peter not having enough faith, which of course, is part of the message. But how about the fact that before he sank, he had enough faith to even start walking! And he did, "until" he took his eyes off Jesus. So when Peter had his eyes on The Lord, he literally walked on water. But the moment he looked at his surroundings and circumstances, he started to drown. And that is why we must be diligent about keeping our eyes on The Lord so we don't have to drown in the troubles of life anymore.

Don't get me wrong, we will definitely still have troubles on this side of heaven. But let us remember what Jesus said in The Book Of John:

"These things I have spoken unto you, that in me ye might have peace. In the world, ye shall have tribulation, but be of good cheer; I have overcome the world" (John 16:33).

So yes, the troubles will come, but we no longer have to fear them, as The One who overcame the world is with us and loves us for eternity!

As we close this chapter, I'd like to share a little poem that I just came up with. Remember we are fighting 'from' victory, not 'for'it!

When darkness hovered the whole worldwide, God created light and shoved it aside. When Jesus was brutally slain on that Tree, the devil was defeated for the whole world to see. When our thoughts are so painful and it seems like the end, our great Savior is with us, our One True Friend. So do not fear when the battle is tough. God's love is everlasting and more than enough. When the devil whispers sweet lies in your ear, call out to Jesus. He is always right here. When you feel so insane and all hope is lost, lay that all down at the foot of the Cross. The battle is real and sometimes so hard to tell. But we have a heaven that defeats any hell. And when we give all our life to Christ, we only die once and never die twice. So never give up, you have already won. Just believe it, receive it because of God's Son. Soon will be a day with no darkness, no tears. No devil, no demons, no hatred, no fears. But while we're still here, if we focus on Him, the darkness still comes but will slowly grow dim. And the closer we get to His triumphant return; the world will fade but never His Word. Until that day comes, let's live out His love by setting our minds on things above!"

DIVE DEEPER:

Read 2 Corinthians 10:1

- What are the weapons that we have that Paul speaks of in this verse?

- How are they contrary to the world's weapons?

- What are some ways you tried to fight your battles without the Word?

- Did those strategies ever truly work?

KEY THOUGHT:

When we fight with the Word, we will win every battle.

THINK ON THESE THINGS:

Try to memorize and meditate on 2 Corinthians 10:1.

POWER PRAYER:

Lord, I am tired of losing my battles and being attacked by the devil. Forgive me when I try to fight in my own strength. But from this day forward, I ask You to fight my battles with and for me and help me use the Weapon of Your Word to help me do so. In the Name of the King of All Kings, Jesus Amen.

CHAPTER 14

DEFEATING DEPRESSION WITH THE WORD

FINDING HOPE IN THE WORD OF GOD

The LORD is close to the brokenhearted; he rescues those whose spirits are crushed Psalm 34:18

Before you begin this chapter please please know, that this does not negate seeing a doctor or being on medication. Please do so if you need to. But with that said we know God can and does work through both of those avenues and His Word is more powerful than all. So those are definitely great forms of help, but our ultimate help is in Him and His Word!

As you navigate the turbulent waters of depression, it's essential to understand that the battle is not only in your mind but also in your spirit. One powerful tool at your disposal is the Word of God, a source of wisdom, comfort, and strength.

THE POWER OF SCRIPTURE

The Bible, as the Word of God, is a wellspring of hope and healing. In times of depression, you may feel lost, isolated, and overwhelmed. Yet, within the pages of this ancient text lies a timeless message of love, redemption, and transformation.

One verse that has provided solace to countless individuals is found in the book of Psalms, Chapter 34, verse 18: "The Lord is close to the brokenhearted and saves those who are crushed in spirit." This verse reminds us that even in our darkest moments, God is near, ready to provide comfort and rescue.

RENEWING YOUR MIND

To overcome depression, it's essential to renew your mind with the truths found in the Bible. Romans 12:2 instructs us,

> *"Do not conform to the pattern of this world but be transformed by the renewing of your mind."*

This renewal involves immersing yourself in the Word of God and allowing its life-changing truths to replace the negative thought patterns that often accompany depression.

Start by setting aside time each day to read and meditate on Scripture. You can begin with passages that specifically address the issues you're facing. For instance, if you're battling feelings of worthlessness, consider meditating on Ephesians 2:10, which reminds you that you are God's "workmanship, created in Christ Jesus for good works."

THE POWER OF DECLARATIONS

Incorporating Scripture into your daily life doesn't stop with reading; it extends to speaking. Proclaiming biblical truths can be a powerful way to combat depressive thoughts. For instance, if anxiety plagues your mind, recite Philippians 4:6 7:

"Do not be anxious about anything, but in everything by prayer and supplication with thanksgiving let your requests be made known to God. And the peace of God, which surpasses all

understanding, will guard your hearts and your minds in Christ Jesus."

By speaking these verses, you're reinforcing the positive and faith-building aspects of your mind, pushing out the negativity that depression seeks to implant.

COMMUNITY AND SUPPORT

Depression can make you feel isolated, but the Bible encourages us to find strength in community. Hebrews 10:24-25 reminds us,

"And let us consider how we may spur one another on toward love and good deeds, not giving up meeting together, as some are in the habit of doing, but encouraging one another."

Seek out a support system within your church or local community. Share your struggles, pray together, and study the Word of God collectively. In these moments of fellowship, you'll find encouragement, understanding, and the hope that is essential for overcoming.

IN CONCLUSION

Depression is a formidable adversary, but it is not invincible. The Word of God serves as a powerful weapon in your battle, offering hope, renewal, and strength. By immersing yourself in Scripture, declaring its truths, and seeking support within a community of believers, you can move toward healing and restoration, knowing that God's love and grace are ever present, even in the midst of your darkest hour.

DIVE DEEPER

Read Psalm 34:18

- Have you ever been crushed in your spirit? If so, what are some ways you have dealt with it?

- Does it encourage you that the Lord is near to the broken-hearted? Why or why not?

- When is the last time you sat with the Lord and just literally broke down in His presence?

- How did you feel when you did so? Explain.

KEY THOUGHT

Just because I don't always feel God's presence does not mean He is not here with me.

THINK ON THESE THINGS

Try to memorize and meditate on Psalm 34:18.

POWER PRAYER

Father, sometimes the anxieties of this world literally break me down and tear my soul. Please help me to know that no matter what this life may bring, You are always with me. And please help me really feel Your presence as much as You will. In the Name above all names, Jesus. Amen.

CHAPTER 15
LOVE IS THE GOAT

If I speak in the tongues of men and of angels, but have not love, I am only a resounding gong or a clanging cymbal. If I have the gift of prophecy and can fathom all mysteries and all knowledge, and if I have a faith that can move mountains, but have not love, I am nothing If I give all I possess to the poor and surrender my body to the flames, but have not love, I gain nothing Love is patient, love is kind. It does not envy, it does not boast, it is not proud It is not rude, it is not self-seeking, it is not easily angered, it keeps no record of wrongs. Love does not delight in evil but rejoices with the truth It always protects, always trusts, always hopes, always perseveres Love never fails. But where there are prophecies, they will cease; where there are tongues, they will be stilled; where there is knowledge, it will pass away.For we know in part and we prophesy in part.But when perfection comes, the imperfect disappears.When I was a child, I talked like a child, I thought like a child, I reasoned like a child. When I became a man, I put childish ways behind me. Now we see but a poor reflection as in a mirror; then we shall see face to face. Now I know in part; then I shall know fully, even as I And now these three remain: faith, hope, and love. But the greatest of these is love (1 Corinthians 13:1-13).

I am quite a rare breed. Please don't hate me or stop reading this book for what I am about to say. But I was and am not a big Beatles fan. But I do love the song "I wanna hold your hand."

With that said, they were right about one thing. "All you need is love."

Dear friends, let us love one another, for love comes from God. Everyone who loves has been born of God and knows God (1 John 4:7-11).

Whoever does not love does not know God because God is love (1 John 4:8).

Dear friends, since God so loved us, we also ought to love one another (1 John 4:11).

A lot of times when we think of love, we think of falling head over heels for our first love. When our knees are shaky and we have that butterfly feeling in our stomachs. Although that is a part of love, True love is so much more than that! Love can show itself in many forms. It could be washing the dishes for your husband or wife when they are just too tired to do it. Or changing your baby's diaper 10 times throughout the day. Or just the simple fact of telling someone you love them, which honestly seems to be a hard thing for most in today's culture.

So yes, love feels amazing at times, but a love also pushes through when that amazing feeling is not always present. But the reward of giving love is so much greater than all the challenges we go through to show it.

"In everything I did, I showed you that by this kind of hard work, we must help the weak, remembering the words the Lord Jesus himself said: 'It is more blessed to give than to receive'" (Acts 20:35).

Love is so important that it is in the top two commandments of the law:

"Love the Lord your God with all your heart and with all your soul and with all your mind.' This is the first and greatest commandment. And the second is like it: 'Love your neighbor as yourself.' All the Law and the Prophets hang on these two commandments" (Matthew 22:37-40).

Everything we are and do starts with God's love:

"But God demonstrates his own love for us in this: While we were still sinners, Christ died for us. Since we have now been justified by his blood, how much more shall we be saved from God's wrath through him!" (Romans 5:8-10).

So like Paul said to the Corinthians, we could do many great things, even God things. But if we don't do them in love, it won't matter. One of the toughest parts, I believe, about love, and I believe most of us would agree, is being able to love our enemies.

"You have heard that it was said, 'Love your neighbor and hate your enemy.' But I tell you, love your enemies and pray for those who persecute you, that you may be children of your Father in heaven" (Matthew 5:43-45).

It is so important to know that this verse isn't saying we should become best friends with our enemies or hang out with them. Although that can definitely happen. It also doesn't mean that what they have done to us is right. But what it does mean is that we put them in God's hands and no longer hold their offenses against them. We do not do it for this intention; however, doing this almost always heals us more than the person we prayed for. Also, as Proverbs 25:21-22 states,

"If your enemy is hungry, give him food to eat; if he is thirsty, give him water to drink. In doing this, you will heap burning coals on his head, and the Lord will reward you."

As we come to the renewing of our minds, the love of God is one of, if not the most important attributes we should set our minds on. But let us remember our ultimate goal is not renewing our minds on the things God "does" for us. Although there is a time for that. But rather to meditate on "Who" He is. I hate to admit, but I have observed a sad but very true ordeal as I walk in this world. But the more and more I notice that a lot of unbelievers show so much more love than some in the church. And to me, that is a great tragedy. I don't say this at all to condemn, and Lord knows I have been guilty of it many times myself. But rather it is just the opposite. I say it to motivate us. To show this world what True Love looks like as never before! We have to show them the only Love that can save their soul. The only way we can do this is by abiding and meditating on the love of God ourselves. And the more we do, the more that love will permeate through us onto others! It's time to change the world with one word. Love! Id like to end the chapter of this book with a life changing challenge. Over the next week or so, if you are up for it, please say to yourself over and over, "God loves me." I know we might think, of course, we know that. But I honestly believe we get so lost in trying to live life that we forget this absolute, amazing truth and who we are living this life for. So when you say it, please really let it soak in so much in your mind that it enters deep down in your heart. I am persuaded by God's Word that when we let this truth capture our hearts and minds, we will live and love more than ever before! God loves you!

DIVE DEEPER

Read Matthew 22:37-40

- Look up the Greek biblical definition for the word "heart."

- After looking that up, what do you think it means to love God with all your heart?

- Is there someone in your life that you have not told in a long time that you love them?

- If so, what do you believe is holding you back?

KEY THOUGHT

Life is too short and God is too good for us to not try to love as much and as many as possible, even when it's tough.

THINK ON THESE THINGS

Try to memorize and meditate on Matthew 22:37-40.

POWER PRAYER

Lord, above all else, help me love with all my heart, mind, soul, and every fiber of my being. So much so that it permeates out of me to everyone You put in my life. In Jesus' name, Amen. Selah.

CHAPTER 16

DYING DAILY TO LIVE FULLY

"He must increase, but I must. decrease" (John 3:30).

As we wage war in our minds, we must set our gaze on the things of the Spirit.

"The mind governed by the flesh is death, but the mind governed by the Spirit is life and peace" (Romans 8:6).

Believe it or not, there is a good form of dying, and that is dying to ourselves, the "I" part of me.

"If anyone desires to come after Me, let him deny himself, take up his cross, and follow Me" (Matthew 16:24).

I know for some, when they read that verse, especially the part about denying themselves, they believe that the Christian life is dull and boring. That God doesn't want us to be happy but holy. But I believe you can't be holy if you are not happy and vice versa.

What Jesus is talking about here is denying ourselves of our ways and agendas to give them up for the ones He has planned for us, which is an amazing thing. Because if we were all being honest, I believe we would admit that our ways don't work so well. Why would we need God if we had it all together? But by denying our way of things, we actually become the true version of ourselves through Christ. And we will come to find, as we walk with Him, that we truly wouldn't want to have it "our" way anyway. When our desires match His, that is when we start to live life at its best.

Take delight in the Lord, and he will give you the desires of your heart. (Psalm 37:4).

I don't know about you, but I am tired of the devil stealing and killing and destroying things in my life! By renewing our mind to the Word is when we actually start truly living.

"The thief comes only to steal and kill and destroy; I have come that they may have life, and have it to the full"
(John 10:10).

Most assuredly, I say to you, unless a grain of wheat falls into the ground and dies, it remains alone; but if it dies, it produces much grain. "He who loves his life will lose it, and he who hates his life in this world will keep it for eternal life"
(John 12:24-26).

So, in this sense, dying is a good thing aside from going to be with Jesus. The more we die, the more we live. The more we deny the flesh and walk in the spirit, the more we will become conformed to the image of Christ.

Not to sound morbid at all, but this is one funeral that will bring us great joy. "That you put off, concerning your former conduct, the old man which grows corrupt according to your deceitful lusts, and be renewed in the spirit of your mind, and that you put on the new man which was created according to God, in true righteousness and holiness." So let us die to ourselves and live for Christ.

There is no greater joy than to let Jesus take over through His Holy Spirit! Only then will we truly live the life we were meant to live. When His dreams become our dreams, His ways become our ways, and His life becomes our life. We will look forward to the deaths of our old selves and flourish like never before as our true selves!

"Therefore, if anyone is in Christ, he is a new creation. The old has passed away; behold, the new has come." This means that anyone who belongs to Christ has become a new person. The old life is gone; a new life has begun (2 Corinthians 5:17). So let us die so we might truly live!

DIVE DEEPER

Read Matthew 16:24

- What do you believe dying to yourself means?

- Do you think that means God doesn't want us to enjoy life? Why or why not?

- What are some things you need God to help you deny yourself in your current situation?

KEY THOUGHT

God only holds out on things that will either hurt us or destroy us. He is not a killjoy. In fact, He is the author of true joy.

THINK ON THESE THINGS

Try to memorize and meditate on Matthew 16:24.

POWER PRAYER

Dear Lord, please help me decrease so You can increase in my life. In Jesus' name, Amen.

CHAPTER 17

THE JOY SET BEFORE US

In the midst of the bustling city of Jerusalem, on a hill called Golgotha, a profound and poignant scene unfolded. It was a scene that would echo through the annals of history, a moment of sacrifice and ultimate redemption. These words from the book of Hebrews, "for the joy that was set before him endured the cross, despising the shame, and is set down at the right hand of the throne of God," encapsulate the essence of that moment and the journey that led to it.

The protagonist of this story, Jesus of Nazareth, stood before a cross, bearing the weight of humanity's sins.

The crowd that had once hailed him as a king now mocked him, and the weight of the wooden beam pressed into his wounded shoulders. It was a moment of unbearable physical and emotional pain, but there was something else that sustained him: the joy set before him.

This joy was not the fleeting happiness of earthly success or comfort; it was the fulfillment of a divine purpose. It was the reconciliation of humanity with God, the salvation of souls, and the restoration of broken relationships. It was the redemption of a fallen world. This was the joy that kept him going, even as the world around him seemed to crumble.

In despising the shame, Jesus exhibited a profound understanding of the bigger picture. The shame of the cross was immense, for it was the symbol of humiliation and suffering. Yet, in his heart, he despised that shame because he knew it was but a shadow compared to the eternal glory that awaited him. The shame of the cross was the gateway to the exaltation at the right hand of the throne of God.

As Jesus hung there, the heavens darkened, the earth quaked, and the curtain in the temple was torn from top to bottom. It was a cosmic display of the significance of the moment. Jesus had become the sacrificial lamb, the bridge between humanity and God. His sacrifice would make it possible for sinners to approach the throne of God with confidence, seeking forgiveness and redemption.

The journey to that cross was one of unparalleled love, compassion, and sacrifice. It was a journey that culminated in the greatest act of selflessness the world has ever witnessed. And it was this selflessness that would bring about the redemption of humanity.

The verse from Hebrews speaks not only of Jesus' journey but also of the message it conveys to us. It invites us to embrace a joy beyond the temporal, to endure hardship and shame for a higher purpose, and to have faith in the ultimate redemption that awaits those who walk in the footsteps of the one who endured the cross. In our own lives, we can find inspiration in these words, as they remind us that there is meaning and purpose in enduring challenges for the greater good.

DIVE DEEPER

Read Hebrews 12:2-3

⊙ What do you believe was the joy that was set before Jesus?

- What does it mean that He despised the shame?

- If you knew you could live in joy all the days of your life, even when things get bad, how would that change your perspective?

- Look up the difference between happiness and joy.

KEY THOUGHT

God is not a killjoy. He is the ultimate source of joy.

THINK ON THESE THINGS

Try to memorize and meditate on Hebrews 12:2-3.

POWER PRAYER

Lord, please forgive me when I've looked to anything else for joy other than You. You say in Your presence is fullness of joy. Please let me stay in Your presence now and forevermore. In Jesus' name, Amen.

CHAPTER 18

I FINISHED THE RACE

"Soldiering On and Finishing the Race"

"No soldier in active service entangles himself in the affairs of everyday life so that he may please the one who enlisted him as a soldier."(2 Timothy 2:4)

"I have fought the good fight, I have finished the race, I have kept the faith." (2 Timothy 4:7)

INTRODUCTION:

The two verses from 2 Timothy offer valuable insights into the Christian journey. In the first, Paul draws an analogy between a soldier's commitment and our duty as believers. The second verse reflects Paul's own personal testimony near the end of his life. These verses encapsulate the essence of what it means to be a faithful Christian—dedication, endurance, and unwavering faith. Let's explore these verses and the lessons they hold for us.

PART 1: "NO SOLDIER IN ACTIVE SERVICE"

In 2 Timothy 2:4, Paul uses a military metaphor to describe the life of a Christian. He likens our faith journey to that of a dedicated soldier. Just as a soldier's full commitment is to the service of their country, so should a Christian's allegiance be to God.

- *Dedication*: Just as a soldier prioritizes their duty above personal concerns, we must dedicate ourselves to the cause of Christ. This means being intentional about our faith and living with a sense of purpose.

- *Avoiding Entanglements*: A soldier in active service must avoid becoming entangled in civilian matters. Likewise, we should steer clear of worldly distractions that can hinder our spiritual growth.

- *Pleasing Our Enlisting Officer*: The soldier aims to please their commanding officer. For Christians, our ultimate goal is to please God. Our actions, decisions, and conduct should reflect this unwavering devotion.

PART 2: "I HAVE FOUGHT THE GOOD FIGHT"

In 2 Timothy 4:7, Paul reflects on his own journey as a Christian and as a minister of the gospel. He uses the language of a fighter who has persevered and remained faithful to the end.

- *Fought the Good Fight:* Paul's life was marked by spiritual battles and challenges. He had faced opposition, hardships, and trials. But he didn't just fight; he fought the "good" fight—the fight of faith, righteousness, and truth.

Finished the Race: Paul's race wasn't about sprinting but enduring. He didn't give up midway; he completed the race. As Christians, we are called to persevere, no matter how long the journey or how tough the terrain. – Kept the Faith: Paul's unwavering faith was his greatest accomplishment. Through all the trials and tribulations, his trust in God remained steadfast. We too are called to hold onto our faith, even in the face of adversity.

CONCLUSION:

The combination of 2 Timothy 2:4 and 4:7 presents a comprehensive picture of the Christian life. We are called to be dedicated soldiers, putting God first and avoiding worldly entanglements. At the end of our journey, like Paul, we can reflect on our lives with the confidence that we have fought the good fight, finished the race, and kept the faith. May these verses inspire us to continue soldiering on and finish our race with unwavering faith in the one who called us

---

DIVE DEEPER

Read 2 Timothy 4:7

- Does it motivate you that Paul compares our walk with God to a race? Why or why not?

- How much would you love to say, like Paul in this verse, these words when you reach the end of your time here on earth?

- If any, what is one thing stopping you from competing in the race?

- Does it comfort you to know that the apostles screwed up just like us at times? Why or why not?

KEY THOUGHT

When I run for me, I lose. When I run for Christ, I win every time.

THINK ON THESE THINGS

Try to memorize and meditate on 2 Timothy 4:7.

POWER PRAYER

Lord, with You I am ready and prepared to fight the good fight. Please let me finish the race and keep the faith with joy in my heart until I meet You face to face. In Jesus' name, Amen.

CHAPTER 19
FAITH ON FIRE (LITERALLY)

W e're all very familiar with Daniel and the lions' den, or Daniel and his God-given gift to interpret dreams, or how he was promoted to be one of the King's right-hand men. Don't get me wrong, I love Daniel and all those amazing stories. But it's kind of sad to me that, at least in most of the places I've been, people easily pass over Daniel's friends, none other than SMA.

Moreover, at Daniel's request, the king appointed Shadrach, Meshach, and Abednego as administrators over the province of Babylon, while Daniel himself remained at the royal court (Daniel 2:49).

Also known by their Hebrew names, Hananiah, Mishael, and Azariah. Honestly, to me, these guys are some of the greatest heroes and testimonials to faith in the Bible!

Before we dive into their story, let us remember that these were not grown men. They were teenage kids with an unquenchable love for God!

So, let's dive into Daniel chapter 3 to find out more about these bravest of the brave souls and what led up to their trial.

"King Nebuchadnezzar made an image of gold, sixty cubits high and six cubits wide,[a] and set it up on the plain of Dura in the

province of Babylon. He then summoned the satraps, prefects, governors, advisers, treasurers, judges, magistrates, and all the other provincial officials to come to the dedication of the image he had set up. So the satraps, prefects, governors, advisers, treasurers, judges, magistrates, and all the other provincial officials assembled for the dedication of the image that King Nebuchadnezzar had set up, and they stood before it."

"Then the herald loudly proclaimed, 'Nations and peoples of every language, this is what you are commanded to do: As soon as you hear the sound of the horn, flute, zither, lyre, harp, pipe, and all kinds of music, you must fall down and worship the image of gold that King Nebuchadnezzar has set up. Whoever does not fall down and worship will immediately be thrown into a blazing furnace.'"

I speak for myself and any of you who might agree. Although not always intentionally, but I can't help but think, what if I replaced that statue with my phone or my worldly status and what other people think of me? Or worst of all, myself. In honesty, I believe all of us, at one point or another, have had that proverbial statue in our lives. Not saying we always admittedly bow down to our phones or others or to ourselves, but I believe we would all agree that at some point, we have given those things more credence and time than our devotion to God. Literally no judgment whatsoever; I would be the last. But I say this with all the love in my heart. But let us break those statues down (not literally, of course) and like Hebrews 4:16 states, *"Let us, therefore, come boldly to the throne of grace that we may obtain mercy and find grace to help in time of need."*

So back to SMA, Shadrach, Meshach, and Abednego. They were instructed like everyone else present to bow down to the golden statue. The Bible reads on:

"Therefore, as soon as they heard the sound of the horn, flute, zither, lyre, harp, and all kinds of music, all the nations and peoples of every language fell down and worshiped the image of gold that King Nebuchadnezzar had set up."

At this time, some astrologers[c] came forward and denounced the Jews. They said to King Nebuchadnezzar, "May the king live forever! Your Majesty has issued a decree that everyone who hears the sound of the horn, flute, zither, lyre, harp, pipe, and all kinds of music must fall down and worship the image of gold, and that whoever does not fall down and worship will be thrown into a blazing furnace. But there are some Jews whom you have set over the affairs of the province of Babylon—Shadrach, Meshach, and Abednego—who pay no attention to you, Your Majesty. They neither serve your gods nor worship the image of gold you have set up."

Is It possible that maybe SMA didn't hear the command or were just slow to respond? Let's read on.

"Furious with rage, Nebuchadnezzar summoned Shadrach, Meshach, and Abednego. So these men were brought before the king, and Nebuchadnezzar said to them, 'Is it true, Shadrach, Meshach, and Abednego, that you do not serve my gods or worship the image of gold I have set up? Now when you hear the sound of the horn, flute, zither, lyre, harp, pipe, and all kinds of music, if you are ready to fall down and worship the image I made, very good. But if you do not worship it, you will be thrown immediately into a blazing furnace.

Then what god will be able to rescue you from my hand?'"

No, they definitely heard it. But they had something else, or should I say Someone else, on their minds. If this next part of the story doesn't fire you up (not literally), I truthfully don't know what will!

Shadrach, Meshach, and Abednego replied to him,

"King Nebuchadnezzar, we do not need to defend ourselves before you in this matter. If we are thrown into the blazing furnace, the God we serve is able to deliver us from it, and he will deliver us[c] from Your Majesty's hand. But even if he does not, we want you to know, Your Majesty, that we will not serve your gods or worship the image of gold you have set up."

Wow! Every time I read that, I literally get chills down my spine! Think again for a moment that these were just young Hebrew kids we are talking about. Listen to the amazing faith in that statement. God will deliver us "but even if He does not"?! What mountains we could move with that type of faith! We could literally change the world with it. I shamefully admit I sometimes don't even have enough faith to get out of bed at times! But these young brave kids were literally about to be thrown into a fiery furnace and possibly end their lives for not bowing down to a stupid statue! But make no mistake, there was nothing stupid about not bowing down to anything other than our Lord! They were ready to give their lives for The One who gave His life for all who would come to Him! And the story even gets more fired up!

Then Nebuchadnezzar was furious with Shadrach, Meshach, and Abednego, and his attitude toward them changed. He ordered the furnace heated seven times hotter than usual and commanded some of the strongest soldiers in his army to tie up Shadrach, Meshach, and Abednego and throw them into the blazing furnace. So these men, wearing their robes, trousers, turbans, and other clothes, were bound and thrown into the blazing furnace. The king's command was so urgent and the furnace so hot and real that it burnt up and killed the King's toughest soldiers.

Yet these teenagers walked into it with one thing on their minds: God and His love for them. The text doesn't say so; I can only speculate. But I'm sure at some point they had some fear. But if so, that fear was highly overshadowed by their faith!

The best part about this whole story is the fourth Man in the fire, none other than Jesus Himself. King Nebuchadnezzar was close but missed it by a mark. He said, "He looks like 'A' son of the 'gods.'" But make no mistake, He is "The" Son of the "One" true God!

So next time you don't feel God's presence or believe He is with you, please remember this story of Shadrach, Meshach, and Abednego. Your fire can be anything, from not having enough money to pay your bills to having so much anxiety that you don't think you'll make it one more day. But remember, there is One who stands with you in the fires of life. So much so that when it is all said and done, you will come out not even smelling like smoke! That is what I call "faith on fire"! He is with you and will never, ever leave you or forsake you, ever!

DIVE DEEPER:

#Read Daniel 3:16-18

- With all honesty, do you believe you would be able to deal with this situation in the way Shadrach, Meshach, and Abednego did? Why or why not?

- What are some things right now or in the past that you have worshipped over God?

- Did those things ever bring you happiness in the end?

- What is one thing you could fast from today that may be hindering your walk? It doesn't have to be food. It could be your phone for an hour or restricting social media time. Replace it with reading the Word or listening to a good sermon. Keep in mind this will not only give you greater joy but will bring you closer to the Source of all joy.

KEY THOUGHT

We become like the thing we worship.

THINK ON THESE THINGS:

Try to memorize and meditate on Daniel 3:16-18.

POWER PRAYER:

Lord, please forgive me when I've worshipped anything or anyone other than You. You are the only One worthy of all admiration and adoration. Please help keep my mind, heart, soul, and everything within me on You and You alone. In Jesus' Name, Amen.

CHAPTER 20
BEING TRULY MINDFUL

In our fast-paced and distracted world, the practice of mindfulness has gained popularity as a way to find inner peace and focus. However, for Christians, true mindfulness goes beyond secular practices. It is rooted in a deep understanding of God's Word and His transformative power. In this chapter, we will explore the foundation of Christian mindfulness and how it aligns with scripture.

RENEWING YOUR MIND WITH GOD'S WORD

Romans 12:2 (NIV) says,

"Do not conform to the pattern of this world, but be transformed by the renewing of your mind. Then you will be able to test and approve what God's will is—his good, pleasing, and perfect will."

This verse is at the heart of Christian mindfulness. Instead of conforming to the world's distractions, we are called to renew our minds with God's truth.

PRAYER AND MEDITATION

Philippians 4:6-7 (NIV) encourages us,

"Do not be anxious about anything, but in every situation, by prayer and petition, with thanksgiving, present your requests to God. And the peace of God, which transcends all understanding, will guard your hearts and your minds in Christ Jesus."

Christian mindfulness involves prayer and meditation on God's Word. This practice connects us with our Heavenly Father and brings His peace into our lives.

BEING PRESENT WITH GOD

Psalm 46:10 (NIV) says,

"Be still, and know that I am God; I will be exalted among the nations, I will be exalted in the earth."

True Christian mindfulness involves being still in God's presence. It's not about emptying our minds but filling them with the knowledge of God's presence.

GUARDING YOUR THOUGHTS

2 Corinthians 10:5 (NIV) advises,

"We demolish arguments and every pretension that sets itself up against the knowledge of God, and we take captive every thought to make it obedient to Christ."

Christian mindfulness is about taking control of your thoughts and ensuring they align with God's truth.

MINDFUL GRATITUDE

Colossians 3:17 (NIV) reminds us,

"And whatever you do, whether in word or deed, do it all in the name of the Lord Jesus, giving thanks to God the Father through him."

Being mindful as a Christian means recognizing and appreciating God's blessings, even in the midst of life's challenges.

CONCLUSION

Christian mindfulness is not about escaping from reality but embracing it with a Christ-centered perspective. By renewing our minds with God's Word, practicing prayer and meditation, being present with God, guarding our thoughts, and maintaining an attitude of gratitude, we can experience the true peace and transformation that comes from a mindful life in Christ.

In the following chapters, we will explore practical techniques and strategies for incorporating Christian mindfulness into your daily life, enabling you to live in a way that honors God and brings you lasting peace and joy.

DIVE DEEPER:

Read Psalm 46:10

- When is the last time you honestly just sat still in the presence of the Lord?

- It doesn't have to be a specific amount of time. Make time in your day, even if it's 5 minutes, and literally just sit or lay still in silence in the presence of God.

- Or just ask Him about one thing on your heart and what He wants for you, and then remain silent and actively listen. You might be very surprised by what you hear or feel. And remember, He is not surprised or disappointed at anything you bring up.

KEY THOUGHT:

For every 10 minutes we talk to the Lord, let us spend 20 minutes listening to Him.

POWER PRAYER:

Dear Lord, with so many distractions in this world or even ones I've brought upon myself, please help me to always find time to be in Your presence and keep my ears wide open. Thank you so much that I can talk and have a relationship with You, the Creator of the universe. There is nothing more exciting than being with and spending time with You, and I can never thank You enough for loving me and hearing my prayers. Please let me hear Your voice like never before! In Jesus' Name, Amen.

CHAPTER 21

CCT (CROSS CENTERED THINKING)

"But may it never be that I would boast, except in the cross of our Lord Jesus Christ, through which the world has been crucified to me, and I to the world." - Galatians 6:14

"For the message of the cross is foolishness to those who are perishing, but to us who are being saved it is the power of God." – 1 Corinthians 1:18

To some, the Cross means death. To others, the cross is offensive, as it forces them to look at themselves and the sins they have committed. Also, to some, it is just merely a symbol. But to us who believe, the Cross of Christ is the center of everything we believe, where our great Savior was nailed to that Tree, where He died for you and for me. At the same time, disarming all the powers of hell and making a public spectacle for all to see! The only way to God! The one and only God!

"But He was wounded for our transgressions, He was bruised for our iniquities; The chastisement for our peace was upon Him, And by His stripes, we are healed." – Isaiah 53:5

If we could sum up the Cross in one word, save Jesus, it would be love!

"Greater love has no one than this: to lay down one's life for one's friends." – John 15:13

"Very rarely will anyone die for a righteous person, though for a good person someone might possibly dare to die." – Romans 5:7-8

But God demonstrates His own love for us in this: While we were still sinners, Christ died for us.

When we set our minds and hearts on Christ and the Cross, no devil in hell will be able to stop God's plans for our lives! When we come to the point like the Apostle Paul did, saying,

"When I came to you, brothers, I did not come with eloquence or superior wisdom as I proclaimed to you the testimony about God. For I resolved to know nothing while I was with you except Jesus Christ and Him crucified. I came to you in weakness and fear, and with much trembling."
– 1 Corinthians 2:1

We can know then that we are on the path to victory and become more than overcomers through Him who loved us!

"For I am persuaded that neither death nor life, nor angels nor principalities nor powers, nor things present nor things to come, nor height nor depth, nor any other created thing, shall be able to separate us from the love of God which is in Christ Jesus our Lord." – Romans 8:37-39

CBT (Cognitive Behavioral Therapy) is mostly world-renowned and is quite an effective method that has been used for years to retrain your brain. As some of you may know, to summarize it, it is basically a form of therapy where you change your negative thoughts to positive ones with the help of a therapist or counselor. It's kind of funny to me, but the Apostle Paul had started "CBT" thousands of years ago as he states in Romans 12:2:

"Do not conform to the pattern of this world, but be transformed by the renewing of your mind. Then you will be able to test and approve what God's will is—His good, pleasing, and perfect will."

The results and statistics of CBT have been quite amazing. However, they are missing one ingredient that changes everything and will change anyone who sets their minds on it. And that is Christ and the Cross. CBT tells you to change your negative to positive. But I am not speaking of positive affirmations or self-talk. What I speak of is greater than any positive influence. Don't get me wrong, it's beyond positive and so much more. But as believers, we go from the negative to the Truth of God's Word. Because no matter how we "feel," the Word is always true. And the more we replace the lies with the Truth, not only will we reap amazing benefits, but the greatest benefit of all is growing closer to our Father!

So with that, I propose a new thought: CCT (Cross Centered Thinking). Please know I am not a medical professional by any means, but I am a person who has searched the Bible for years against the struggles of my life. And I am fully persuaded that focusing on the Cross and Christ with all our hearts, souls, and minds will change us forevermore! So when we look at our circumstances and everything around us is falling apart, come to the Cross. When you hear that negative doctor's report and feel there is no hope, come to the Cross. When you feel like giving up everything and leaving this crazy world behind, come to the Cross! Don't ever give up but rather, give "it" "up" to Him who knows all and loves you with an everlasting love! No darkness, no hell, no devil, no demons, no pain, no sorrow, no destruction, no death, and nothing in this world or the next will ever triumph the Cross of Christ! You were lost, now found. Now lay it all down at the foot of the Cross! Set all your strength, your weaknesses, your love, your mind, your heart, and everything that is within you on the Cross of Christ, and you will never be lost again! Come to the Cross and stay there!"

DIVE DEEPER:

Read John 15:13

- According to this verse and life in general, what is the greatest love?

- Though He is our great Savior, how often do you think of Jesus as your friend?

- Why is the cross of Christ foolish to some people?

- What is one thing you need to lay down at the foot of the Cross today? Don't be afraid. He already knows and is with you.

KEY THOUGHT:

If we want to take a stand in the world, we must first lay down at the foot of the Cross.

POWER PRAYER:

Lord, I can never begin to thank You enough for nailing my sins to the Cross. You laid down Your life for me. Please help me lay down my life for You, for Your Glory and the good of others. In Your Mighty Name, Jesus. Amen.

CHAPTER 22

THE MIND OF CHRIST AND THE FRUIT OF THE SPIRIT

"For who has known or understood the mind (the counsels and purposes) of the Lord so as to guide and instruct Him and give Him knowledge? But we have the mind of Christ (the Messiah) and do hold the thoughts (feelings and purposes) of His heart." – 1 Corinthians 2:16

We all know the popular WWJD: What Would Jesus Do? I forgot where I heard it from, but I like this question better. Rather than asking what Jesus would do, we should ask, what would Jesus have "me" do? Because let's be honest, there are just some things He does that we cannot do. However, the Bible says we have the mind of Christ. At first glance, if you are anything like me, you're thinking there's no way with all the craziness going on in my mind that I have the mind of Christ?! But indeed we do. However, that does not mean we always "operate" with the mind of Jesus. But we do have access to it. We will never gain perfection on this side of heaven. However, as Paul said,

"Not that I have already obtained this or am already perfect, but I press on to make it my own because Christ Jesus has made me his own." – Philippians 3:12.

That, to me, is one of the most amazing benefits we have as believers. That we can never get enough of God, yet we are completely satisfied in Him at the same time! In no other walk of life, could you ever state that. More money, more problems. More God, more joy. And you can replace the word money with anything this world offers, and you would come to the same conclusion. Not by any means saying we don't need money or material things, but definitely saying it's okay to have things as long as they don't have us. But we can never run the well dry of God and His love!

I believe one of the most awesome promises in Scripture is in James 4:8:

"Draw near to God, and He will draw near to you."

I don't know about you, but to me, that is an irresistible offer!

So getting back to having the mind of Christ. The only way to push towards perfection in that area is, of course, by the renewing of the mind to His Word! Because after all, His Word is His thoughts and His ways. And also what He is saying to us. And the more we meditate and reflect on His Word, the more we will operate with the mind of Christ. We will also walk in the fruit of the Spirit.

"But the fruit of the Spirit is love, joy, peace, forbearance, kindness, goodness, faithfulness, gentleness, and self-control. Against such things, there is no law." – Galatians 5:22-23.

I was talking with an unbeliever friend of mine (who I've been praying fervently that she comes to Christ). But she is very liberal. I am by no means debating politics here. In fact, aside from praying for our leaders, I would rather leave that to the politicians. I try my best to stick to God things!

With that said, we started talking about freedom and the whole "we can be whoever we say we are." I know this is a sensitive subject for many. And I say this with all love in my heart. So we talked about the idea of freedom. And sadly, the world's definition of freedom is not freedom at all! Anytime we speak of freedom, we also have to consider the consequences of that freedom. This might not be the greatest analogy, but I believe the point will be made.

I told my friend, I have the freedom right now to smack my head on the concrete. But also said that would be a pretty stupid idea as I could end up dead or have a severe brain injury. But I am completely free to do so if I wanted to. Does that make it right? Is that freedom? Kind of yes. But absolutely, positively not at all! True freedom is actually being under the control of The Holy Spirit and God's love, and the consequences of that are love, joy, peace, patience, kindness, goodness…

"So what freedom would you choose? Of course!

'So if the Son sets you free, you will be free indeed.'
–John 8:36.

True freedom is not doing what our "old" selves wanted to do. Even though currently the old man may be acting up a little as a believer. But our freedom comes through our "new" selves and the things we were actually meant for anyway by walking by the Spirit, so we will not gratify the desires of the flesh.

"No alcohol, no drug, no money, nor anything could give us this kind of joy!

And do not get drunk with wine, for that is debauchery, but [you Christians, who already have the Spirit] be filled with the Spirit, addressing one another in psalms and hymns and spiritual songs, singing and making melody to the Lord with your heart, giving thanks always and for everything to God the Father in the name of our Lord Jesus Christ.

The Spirit-Filled life is the only life worth living and dying for so we can live again with Christ!" When we finally come to the point and realize that nothing in this world, actually nothing at all, could ever satisfy our deepest needs, that is when true life starts to begin! Because God's water never runs dry.

"But whoever drinks of the water that I will give him will never be thirsty again. The water that I will give him will become in him a spring of water welling up to eternal life."
– John 4:14.

If you are still thirsty, drink more of the Lord!

DIVE DEEPER:

Read Galatians 5:22-23

- What is your favorite fruit of the Spirit? Why?

- What do you think it means to have the mind of Christ?

- Pick one fruit of the Spirit you feel called to work on. Of course, ask the Holy Spirit Himself to help you.

KEY THOUGHT:

When we walk in the Spirit, we walk in freedom, as there is no law against it.

THINK ON THESE THINGS:

Try to memorize and meditate on Galatians 5:22-23.

POWER PRAYER:

Father, please help me always walk in the fruit of the Spirit so I don't fulfill the lusts of the flesh. I thank you that I am beyond blessed to have the mind of Your Son. Please help me to always cooperate with and operate in it. In Jesus' Name. Amen.

CHAPTER 23

OVERCOMING THE SNARES OF SATAN

As believers, we are constantly engaged in a spiritual battle against the forces of evil, with Satan as our adversary. The Bible teaches us that one of the most potent weapons in our arsenal is the Word of God. In this chapter, we will explore how we can use the Word of God to overcome the snares and temptations set by Satan.

THE POWER OF GOD'S WORD

The Bible is not just a book; it is a living, breathing source of divine wisdom and guidance. In Hebrews 4:12, we are reminded that "the word of God is living and active, sharper than any two-edged sword." This verse highlights the transformative power of God's Word. It has the ability to pierce through the darkness, discern our thoughts and intentions, and bring clarity to our lives.

ARMOR OF GOD

Ephesians 6:11-12 instructs us to *"Put on the whole armor of God, that you may be able to stand against the schemes of the devil. For we do not wrestle against flesh and blood, but against the rulers, against the authorities, against the cosmic powers over this present darkness." This armor includes the "sword of the Spirit, which is the word of God" (Ephesians 6:17).*

When we equip ourselves with the Word of God, we fortify our spiritual armor. Just as a soldier relies on their sword for protection, we can rely on God's Word to fend off the attacks of the enemy. Satan's snares may come in the form of doubt, temptation, or deception, but the Word of God provides us with truth, faith, and discernment.

RESISTING TEMPTATION

When Jesus faced Satan's temptations in the wilderness, He responded with Scripture (Matthew 4:1-11). By doing so, He demonstrated the power of the Word in resisting the devil. We can follow His example by memorizing and meditating on key passages of Scripture. When we encounter temptations, we can call upon the Word to remind us of God's commands and promises.

RENEWING THE MIND

Romans 12:2 encourages us to "be transformed by the renewal of your mind." The Word of God plays a crucial role in this transformation. When we saturate our minds with Scripture, we begin to think as God thinks. We gain a biblical perspective, which allows us to discern between what is from God and what is from the enemy.

PRAYER AND THE WORD

Prayer is another essential component of overcoming the snares of Satan. It is through prayer that we seek God's guidance, strength, and protection. Pairing prayer with the Word of God creates a powerful synergy. We can pray the Scriptures, using them as the foundation for our conversations with God. This not only strengthens our faith but also connects us intimately with our Creator.

COMMUNITY AND ACCOUNTABILITY

As Christians, we are not meant to walk this journey alone. Having a community of believers who can provide support, encouragement, and accountability is crucial. They can help us stay grounded in the Word, and when we face the snares of Satan, they can remind us of the truths found in Scripture.

In conclusion, the Word of God is a formidable weapon against the snares of Satan. By immersing ourselves in Scripture, wearing the armor of God, resisting temptation, renewing our minds, and combining prayer with the Word, we can effectively navigate the spiritual battlefield. With the Word as our guide, we can overcome the schemes of the enemy and lead lives that honor and glorify our Heavenly Father.

DIVE DEEPER:

Read Hebrews 4:12

- What does it mean that the Word is alive and active?

- Look up the Greek word for alive or life.

- What does it mean to rightly divide the Word of truth?

- Do you like when the Word penetrates even to dividing soul and spirit, joints and marrow? Why or why not?

- Remember, everything God does in us is born out of love, even when things hurt at times.

KEY THOUGHT:

The devil can never win as long as we abide in God's Word.

THINK ON THESE THINGS:

Try to memorize and meditate on Hebrews 4:12.

POWER PRAYER:

Thank you, Lord, for giving me Your Word to destroy the schemes of the devil. Please help me to always respond to his attacks with "it is written" so I can have victory in every battle. In Jesus' Name. Amen.

CHAPTER 24
THE PATH OF PAUL

THE ROAD TO DAMASCUS

In the early years of the Christian church, a figure emerged whose life would have a profound impact on the spread of Christianity. This man was Saul of Tarsus, who later became known as the Apostle Paul. His conversion from a fierce persecutor of Christians to one of the most influential leaders of the early church is a story of transformation and divine intervention that has left an indelible mark on the history of Christianity.

PERSECUTOR OF CHRISTIANS

Saul was born in Tarsus, a city in modern-day Turkey, and was a devout Pharisee. He zealously adhered to the Jewish faith and saw the early Christian movement as a threat to the traditional Jewish beliefs. He actively persecuted and imprisoned Christians, approving of the stoning of Stephen, one of the first Christian martyrs. Saul's reputation as a persecutor of Christians struck fear into the hearts of the early followers of Jesus.

THE JOURNEY TO DAMASCUS

Saul's dramatic transformation began on the road to Damascus. He was on a mission to apprehend and bring back Christians to Jerusalem for trial when, suddenly, a blinding light from heaven surrounded him. He fell to the ground and heard a voice saying, "Saul, Saul, why are you persecuting me?" He responded, "Who are you, Lord?" The voice replied, "I am Jesus, whom you are persecuting."

THE BLINDING REVELATION

This encounter with the risen Christ was a turning point in Saul's life. The blinding light and the words of Jesus had a profound impact on him. He realized that the Christians he was persecuting were followers of the Messiah, and that he had been persecuting the very Son of God. Saul's physical blindness mirrored his spiritual blindness, and it became a symbol of his need for transformation.

ANANIAS' ROLE

In Damascus, Saul was blind and in shock. The Lord instructed a devout Christian named Ananias to go to Saul and lay hands on him to restore his sight. Ananias was understandably hesitant, as he knew of Saul's reputation, but he obeyed the Lord's command. When he laid hands on Saul, something like scales fell from his eyes, and he regained his sight.

TRANSFORMATION AND BAPTISM

Saul's transformation was not only physical but also spiritual. He immediately began to preach about Jesus in the synagogues, proclaiming that Jesus was the Son of God. This astonished those who knew him as a persecutor of Christians. He had a new perspective, and his understanding of the Scriptures was profoundly changed.

After his conversion, Saul became known as Paul and devoted his life to spreading the message of Christ to both Jews and Gentiles. His extensive missionary journeys, recorded in the New Testament, led to the establishment of Christian communities throughout the Roman world. Paul's letters, known as the Epistles, became a significant part of the New Testament and provided essential theological insights for the early church.

CONCLUSION

The conversion of the Apostle Paul is a remarkable example of how a person's life and beliefs can be completely transformed by a divine encounter. His journey from a persecutor of Christians to a passionate preacher of the Gospel underscores the power of faith and the enduring message of Christ's grace and forgiveness. Paul's life and writings continue to inspire Christians around the world, reminding them that no one is beyond the reach of God's transformative love and grace.

DIVE DEEPER:

Read Acts 26:14

- Like Paul, do you ever feel like you are fighting with yourself in your walk? Why or why not?

- Have you ever found yourself doing something that you honestly thought was for God, but discovered later on that it wasn't?

- Like Ananias was to Paul, is there someone in your life that you have had contention with but felt led by the Spirit to lay your hands on, either proverbially or literally? Ask the Holy Spirit for the courage and motivation to do so.

KEY THOUGHT:

Just because we are doing something for "good" doesn't always mean it's for God.

POWER PRAYER:

Lord, like Paul, I was once blind. But because of Your grace and goodness, I can now see. I can never thank You enough. But also like Paul, I pray that as I walk with You, You continue to pull the scales off my eyes so I can walk rightly and righteously in the glorious Name of Jesus. Amen

CHAPTER 25

WANNA BE LIKE CHRIST

"For whom He did foreknow, He also did predestinate to be conformed to the image of His Son, that He might be the firstborn among many brethren (Romans 8:29).

As we draw to the close of this book, I believe by now that you understand how important it is to renew our minds to God's Word. One of the main goals of renewing your mind, aside from thinking like Christ, is to ultimately bear the image of Christ Himself.

Anyone who grew up or was around in the '90s is most likely familiar with the famous song about Michael Jordan: "Wanna be like Mike." I will spare you from me writing out all the lyrics, but I'd like to share a few. The opening line is "sometimes I dream that he is me." And then a little later on it sings "I dream I knew, I dream I grew like Mike if I could be like Mike." Now, just to have some fun, as I have to admit, it's quite a catchy song. Please look up the video on Youtube.. All I ask is that you replace "Mike" with "Christ." If you are anything like me, you'll be singing this song for at least the next few weeks or so!

But in all seriousness, that is our ultimate goal in sanctification. Thinking like Christ. Acting like Christ.

Being like Christ and loving like Christ. And it all starts by the renewing of the mind to The Word of Christ. Let us, with great strength and confidence, finally silence the lies of the enemy and tear down the strongholds that divide our minds by renewing our minds like never before!

I must warn you, as you begin to fight this battle, you will most likely face great opposition, as the devil despises God's children who grow closer to Him. But let us never forget! 1 John 4:4 –

"You, dear children, are from God and have overcome them because the one who is in you is greater than the one who is in the world."

And let us also remember Romans 8:11 –

"The Spirit of God, who raised Jesus from the dead, lives in you. And just as God raised Christ Jesus from the dead, He will give life to your mortal bodies by this same Spirit living within you."

If you meditate on one thing from this book, please meditate on that verse! You have the same Spirit that raised Christ from the dead living inside you?! Can you imagine how much we could do for the kingdom if all of us as believers walked with that truth, confident in our minds all day long?! What a great victory it would be and can be!

So when all hell breaks loose, and your mind is spiraling with a million negative thoughts, or you feel that happiness and joy are so far out of reach that you will never find them, or when you hear the negative doctor's report, or you just can't take this crazy world anymore and feel there is no way out, please, please, I beseech with all that is within me,

"Set your minds on things above, not on earthly things"
(Colossians 3:2).

For you died, and your life is now hidden with Christ in God, and you will win the greatest battle that has ever been fought! It is written! If we could be like Christ. God bless you and thank you so much for coming on this journey with me! I pray with all my heart that you renew your mind to The Word of God like never before! That you silence the lies of Satan. That you find the peace and joy that only God can give! So set your mind on things above and let us change the world with God's love!

DIVE DEEPER:

Read 1 John 4:4

- Who is the first "He" that this verse refers to? And who is the second "he" (lowercase h)?

- Imagine how much your life would change if you walked with the confidence every day that you have the same power inside you that raised Christ from the dead. You do, and please don't ever forget that!

- With God and His Word, by renewing your mind, you can literally overcome any obstacle the devil tries to destroy you with. Through Christ, you are more than an overcomer. You are a blood-bought child of God who will fear no evil, come boldly to the throne, and thought by thought take back the years that the enemy has stolen! Believe it, love it, live it, and like Nike, just do it!

- God is with you, and greater is He who is in you than he who is in the world!

- Never give up on God because regardless, He will never give up on you! From this day forward, declare that you will set your mind on things above. You will fight the good fight, you will finish the race, and no devil in hell will be able to stop you!

CONCLUSION

Action Plan For Renewing Your Mind

1. *Regular Bible study and meditation:* Set aside dedicated time each day to read and study the Bible. Use resources like commentaries or study guides to gain a deeper understanding of the text.

2. *Scripture memorization:* Choose verses or passages that resonate with you and commit them to memory.

   Repeat them often throughout the day to keep them at the forefront of your mind.

3. *Daily affirmations*: Create positive affirmations based on biblical principles and repeat them to yourself regularly. For example, "I am loved and cherished by God," or "I am fearfully and wonderfully made."

4. *Surround yourself with like-minded individuals:* Join a Bible study group or a church community where you can discuss and learn from others who are also focused on renewing their minds with the Word of God.

5. *Listen to Christian podcasts or sermons:* Find reputable Christian speakers or preachers who deliver messages aligned with biblical teachings. Listen to these podcasts or sermons regularly to hear practical applications of the Word of God.

6. *Journaling*: Start a journal where you can reflect on your readings and record any insights, questions, or lessons learned. Write down prayers and record instances where you see God's work in your life.

7. *Practice mindfulness and gratitude:* Incorporate gratitude into your daily routine present in the moment and focus on God's goodness and faithfulness.

8. *Engage in spiritual disciplines:* Participate in activities like fasting, solitude, or silence to draw closer to God and deepen your connection with Him.

9. *Serve others:* Actively seek opportunities to serve and help others, as Jesus taught. Volunteering at a local charity or church, visiting the sick or elderly, or participating in outreach programs can help you internalize the values of love, compassion, and selflessness found in the Word of God.

10. *Seek guidance through prayer:* Regularly pray to God for wisdom, discernment, and guidance. Ask the Holy Spirit to illuminate the Word of God and reveal its meaning and application in your life.

ADDITIONAL RESOURCE

Daily Biblical Affirmations To Start Your Day Right

Here's a list of daily biblical affirmations about happiness:

1. "Rejoice in the Lord always; again I will say, rejoice!" – Philippians 4:4

2. "Delight yourself in the Lord, and he will give you the desires of your heart." – Psalm 37:4

3. "The Lord is my strength and my shield; my heart trusts in him, and I am helped. Therefore my heart exults, and with my song I shall thank him." – Psalm 28:7

4. "May the God of hope fill you with all joy and peace as you trust in him, so that you may overflow with hope by the power of the Holy Spirit." – Romans 15:13

5. "This is the day that the Lord has made; let us rejoice and be glad in it." – Psalm 118:24

6. "The joy of the Lord is your strength." – Nehemiah 8:10

7. "Blessed are those who hunger and thirst for righteousness, for they shall be satisfied." – Matthew 5:6

8. "You will make known to me the path of life; in your presence is fullness of joy; in your right hand, there are pleasures forever." – Psalm 16:11

9. "I will rejoice and be glad in your steadfast love because you have seen my affliction; you have known the distress of my soul." – Psalm 31:7

10. "Restore to me the joy of your salvation, and uphold me with a willing spirit." – Psalm 51:12

I hope these affirmations bring you happiness and peace in your daily life! There is no greater Joy than being in The Word! God bless you and He loves you more than you'll ever know!

ABOUT THE AUTHOR